Few books have the potential to change your life as much as this one. I found it personally encouraging and challenging at the same time—a profound and practical reservoir of wisdom. Don't just read it. Highlight it, underline it, and most of all, implement its teachings in your life. Transformation awaits!

LEE STROBEL, *New York Times* bestselling author of *The Case for Christ* and *The Case for Miracles*

It's strange to describe a book on self-control as compulsively readable, but that's how it is. I had no idea that learning how to get a grip on myself could be so enlightening, inspiring, and flat-out entertaining. And helpful, to boot. But that's how it is. Drew Dyck's latest work is a page-turner and an eye-opener. I simply couldn't muster enough self-control to put it down. But before you judge me, you try, and see how well you do.

MARK BUCHANAN, author, *Your Church Is Too Safe*

It isn't an overstatement to say that nearly everything ailing our society, our communities, our families, and ourselves is rooted in our lack of self-control. In the past we celebrated the virtues of self-discipline and self-sacrifice. Those days are over. Now virtually everything in our culture celebrates self-centeredness and encourages us to satisfy every desire. Where our culture has failed us, however, Drew Dyck has stepped into the breach. His book is a winsome and important exploration of the forgotten virtue that has been foundational to the Christian life, and to free societies, for two millennia. This is a conversation more Christian communities need to be having, and Dyck is the right voice to start it.

SKYE JETHANI, award-winning author and cohost of *The Holy Post* podcast

This book was exactly what I wanted it to be: Big Science + Deep Bible + Practical Next Steps. I love what Drew has done here!

JON ACUFF, *New York Times* bestselling author of *Finish: Give Yourself the Gift of Done*

Here's the straight up truth: you need to read this book. The only thing wrong with this book is that it wasn't written and handed to me when I was a teenager! Drew Dyck's newest book is necessary on every level. Not only is this book true and practical, it's a lot of fun! Drew has a winsome way of explaining things that make the book a pleasure to read. I plan on getting this book into the hands of everyone I know.

DANIEL FUSCO, pastor of Crossroads Community Church, Author, *Upward, Inward, Outward: Love God, Love Yourself, Love Others*

This book is perfect for the times we are living in. Society tells us to go for the instant gratification. "It's all about you! If it feels good, do it!" Yet on the whole, I don't know if we have ever been more unfulfilled or restless. This book convincingly presents the opposite viewpoint—that discipline is the path to contentment. Of course that's easier said than done. I appreciated the author's self-effacing tone, and his invitation to ride shotgun on his personal road trip to discovering the ability and virtue of self-control. The truths this book uncovers about this all-important character trait give hope to all of us. Read *Your Future Self Will Thank You* because your future self really will thank you.

MATT BIRK, former NFL player and Super Bowl C

Self-control is something we all need but not somet ____ ____ _re
Self Will Thank You, Drew Dyck pulls back the curt ____ ____ us
to help (and the Helper). Your future self will thank

TRILLIA NEWBELL, author, *If God is For Us, Fear ana ____ ____ ery Good Idea*

Over the past decade, researchers have developed a rich understanding of how self-control really works. They've answered questions such as how to get more of it, how to best use it, and what depletes it. In this important book, my friend Drew Dyck does a great job of making sense of what this research means for Christians. He engages it with a biblical worldview, and tells us what we need to know to live more fruitful lives of more self-control. Well done!

BRADLEY WRIGHT, sociologist, University of Connecticut; author, *Upside: Surprising Good News About the State of Our World*

This book will not beat you up, but it won't make you feel warm and fuzzy. Instead, it is a gospel-saturated, science-based approach to stewarding your life. Drew Dyck is one of the most arresting writers in the evangelical world. So go get this book today. It will be the one impulse buy you won't regret!

DANIEL DARLING, Communications VP at Ethics and Religion Liberty Commission; author, *The Dignity Revolution: Reclaiming God's Rich Vision for Humanity*

Drew Dyck writes with candor, humor, and urgency about a subject that has never been more essential, but more elusive than it is today—the importance of self-control. Y*our Future Self Will Thank You* is a well-researched, accessible, and practical book about one of the Bible's most central but most overlooked principles for living a godly, joyful, and purposeful life.

KARL VATERS, author, *Small Church Essentials* and *The Grasshopper Myth*

In our cultural moment, I cannot think of many subjects more in need of discussion than self-control. And I can't think of a better person to lead that discussion than Drew Dyck. Dyck's winsome voice pairs approachability with theological clarity and direct exhortation. He made me smile and see my own folly at the same time. I have much to learn on the subject of self-control, which makes me especially thankful for this book.

RUSS RAMSEY, pastor of Christ Presbyterian Church Cool Springs; author, Retelling the Story Series

Okay, I'll admit it: I procrastinated picking up this book. But was so glad when I did! *Your Future Self Will Thank You* combines rich biblical insight, fascinating scientific research, and on-the-ground practical wisdom on the nature of self-control and how to integrate it into your life. While temptations and distractions are everywhere in our digital age, Drew Dyck invites us—with humor, wit, and a lot of vulnerability—to join him on a journey of transformation that ultimately empowers us to better love God, others . . . and our future self.

JOSHUA RYAN BUTLER, pastor of Redemption Church; author, *The Skeletons in God's Closet* and *The Pursuing God*

Your Future Self Will Thank You is a practical manual and insightful field-guide to living a productive, fruitful life. With a mixture of informative psychological studies, interviews, biblical wisdom, and personal stories, Drew Dyck has written an incredible resource to help you create a life-giving future story.

PAUL ANGONE, author, *101 Questions You Need to Ask in Your Twenties (And Let's Be Honest, Your Thirties Too)*

Your Future Self Will Thank You

Secrets to Self-Control from the Bible and Brain Science (A Guide for Sinners, Quitters, and Procrastinators)

DREW DYCK

MOODY PUBLISHERS

CHICAGO

Edited by Connor Sterchi
Interior design: Ragont Design
Author photo: Phil Marcelo
Cover design: Erik M. Peterson
Cover photo of French bulldog copyright © 2018 by retales botijero/Getty Images (112041547). All rights reserved.

Library of Congress Cataloging-in-Publication Data

Names: Dyck, Drew, author.
Title: Your future self will thank you : secrets to self-control from the
  Bible and brain science (a guide for sinners, quitters, and
  procrastinators).
Description: Chicago : Moody Publishers, 2019. | Includes bibliographical
  references.
Identifiers: LCCN 2018043345 (print) | LCCN 2019002388 (ebook) | ISBN
  9780802496744 (ebook) | ISBN 9780802418296
Subjects: LCSH: Self-control--Religious aspects--Christianity.
Classification: LCC BV4647.S39 (ebook) | LCC BV4647.S39 D93 2019 (print) |
  DDC 241/.4--dc23
LC record available at https://lccn.loc.gov/2018043345

We hope you enjoy this book from Moody Publishers. Our goal is to provide high-quality, thought-provoking books and products that connect truth to your real needs and challenges. For more information on other books and products written and produced from a biblical perspective, go to www.moodypublishers.com or write to:

Moody Publishers
820 N. LaSalle Boulevard
Chicago, IL 60610

3 5 7 9 10 8 6 4

Printed in the United States of America

To my beloved boy, Athanasius

We gave you a big name. Stick close to Jesus, develop self-control, and I promise, you'll grow into it.

Contents

A Foundation for the Soul

Why I Need This Book More Than You Do

> *Your future self will always see your present self as unwise and immature. That means you are currently a fool right now.*
>
> —TIM KELLER

I make the same resolutions every year.

In case you missed the confession in that first sentence, let me point it out for you. Making the same goals every year usually means you *failed* the year before. But self-improvement is a persistent mistress. By the time New Year's rolls around, I'm ready to renew my vows to a better future.

> *Exercise five times a week.*
> *Lose twenty pounds.*
> *Stick to the budget.*

Not all my failures are health and finance related. Spiritual goals have a tendency to languish on my fridge as well.

> *Pray for fifteen minutes every morning.*

Read through the Bible in one year.
Volunteer in a new role at church.

After recording these goals, I close my Moleskine notebook with a sense of anticipation and pride. I'm almost jealous of my future self. He's going to be so skinny . . . and spiritual! I'm confident about my goals. I feel like they are laudable, and if the literature on goal setting is to be believed, accomplishable. They're concrete, measurable, and (you would think) realistic.

Yet somehow I find myself failing to meet them, year after year after year. And it doesn't take months for my resolutions to unravel. It takes weeks. Days, even.

What's going on?

On one hand, it isn't much of a mystery. I'm the victim of a phenomenon as predictable as it is frustrating. Planning is easy; execution is hard. Anyone can sign up to run a marathon. Propelling your body over 26.2 miles of concrete is where things get rough (or so I'm told). The same is true of just about anything worth doing: it requires a good deal of effort. And most of us fail to follow through, despite our good intentions. As the witty football coach Lou Holtz once remarked, "After all is said and done, more is said than done." If there's anything unique about me, it's not that I fail to meet my goals. It's that I'm continually surprised when I trip over the gap between what I plan to do and what I'm able to accomplish.

> **I'm caught in my own civil war between the good I want to do and the sinful impulses holding me back.**

Of course, not all resolution-breakers are colossal failures in every area of life. I'm not. I strive to be a good husband and father. I'm gainfully employed. I have two degrees and even a couple of books to my name. Heck, I had enough willpower to squeeze out the words you're currently reading (though you wouldn't believe the lollygagging and avoidance behavior that preceded the actual writing).

On the spiritual front, I'm not a total loser either. I go to church most Sundays and my closet is free of skeletons. I give to good causes. I'm assiduous in my study of theology (though embarrassingly inconsistent with Bible reading).

And yet my failure to meet my goals—and not just ones made on New Year's Eve—haunts me, especially when failing to do so has serious consequences.

STUCK IN REVERSE

My brother Darren recently had a heart attack at forty-four years old. Thankfully he quickly got to the hospital, where they threaded a thin tube through a vein in his wrist up to a blocked artery and restored blood flow to his heart. As the shock wore off and we all breathed a sigh of relief that he was going to be okay, I started to think about my own health. When it comes to heart disease, family history is the poor man's genetic testing. When your brother, who is only five years your senior, suffers a heart attack, it's a wakeup call. Or it should be.

I wanted to cut my risk factors, so I hit the ground running. Literally. I fished my Nike running shoes out of the garage and started plodding around my block every evening. My diet got a makeover, too. Burgers and fries were out. Salmon and broccoli were in. I started popping fish oil pills and seeking out foods with

a mysterious component called "fiber." I took a picture of one particularly depressingly healthy meal and texted it to my brother.
"Look at what you're making me do!" I wrote.

I hoped to minimize my risk with diet and exercise, but if I
needed medication, I'd take it. I promised my wife I'd talk to my
doctor. As the father of three young children, I wasn't going to
take any chances. *I guess this is what I needed to take my health
seriously*, I remember thinking. *A good old-fashioned scare.*

But it wasn't. Because a couple of weeks after the new me
emerged, the old me reared his lazy, hungry head. I started
supplementing my healthy meals with handfuls of Doritos each
time I passed the pantry. My jogs around the block dropped in
frequency, and that promised appointment with the doctor kept
getting put off. One night as I sat watching TV eating a bowl of
cookie dough ice cream, I stopped for a moment and thought
what in the world am I doing? . . . and then finished the bowl.

None of these lapses surprise my wife anymore. She shakes
her head every time I announce my plans to go on another diet.
And I've tried them all: one where I counted calories on my
smartphone; another where I restricted eating to only between
2:00 and 6:00 p.m.; another where I limited my intake to only
vegetables and lean meats. Few lasted for more than a week, but
I'm always eager to tackle the latest fad diet that comes along.
It's become something of a joke with friends and family. I'll start
scheming about my next strict eating regimen, even as I fork unhealthy food into my mouth. Between bites, I'll declare, "The diet
starts tomorrow!"

My lack of spiritual resolve is just as vexing. Above I boasted
that I don't have any skeletons in my closet, and it's true. I don't
engage in illegal or scandalous activities. But I say that with the

full realization that many sins I do struggle with—like pride, indifference, averting my eyes from homeless people begging for money—are just as sinister as the ones that make the evening news. Sure, I go to church faithfully. I sing songs with beautiful, inspiring truths. I listen to powerful sermons. Yet year after year, I continue to struggle with the same stupid, stubborn sins. I'm caught in my own civil war between the good I want to do and the sinful impulses holding me back.

Self-control isn't just one good character trait, a nice addition to the pantheon of virtues. It's foundational.

I'll never arrive at perfection, not in this life. I don't expect to. But shouldn't Christians expect to make some progress? Shouldn't they gradually overcome bad habits and besetting sins? Shouldn't they become more humble and selfless? Shouldn't they look a little more like Jesus with every passing year? Shouldn't I?

The reality hit me with extra force the other day when my brother (yes, the heart attack one) posed a difficult question.

"Are you more spiritual today than you were twenty years ago?"

I tried to get off on technicalities.

"Well, I was a teenager then. Plus I've gone to seminary and . . ."

"I'm not talking about how much you *know*," he interrupted.

My brother isn't in the habit of posing deep, difficult questions. Yet he'd posed one nonetheless. It wasn't a sideways confrontation either; he was asking because he was worried about his own lack of growth. His query kept rattling around my skull for the next couple of weeks, and I couldn't shake it out.

In that twenty years, I'd attended church hundreds of times, sang thousands of Christian songs. I'd graduated from seminary. I'd written books. About God! But was I more spiritually mature? Less enslaved to sin? Was I more passionate about following Jesus?

As I look back at my patterns of behaviors and the state of my soul, I don't know if I can say that I am. In many ways, I'm stuck—or even moving in reverse.

FINDING THE FOUNDATION

Around the time I was grappling with my spiritual stuckness, I stumbled upon an intriguing description of a group of ancient Jewish monks. They were called the *Therapeutae* "because, like doctors, they cure and heal the souls of those who come to them or because of their pure and sincere service and worship of the Divine."[1]

And pure it was. The monks led lives of extraordinary discipline and devotion. Their lifestyle was austere in the extreme. Think the TV show *Survivor*, minus the cameras and coups. Renouncing all possessions, they traded city life for caves in the wilderness. They spent their days praying, singing spiritual songs, and meditating on the Hebrew Scriptures. They ate nothing till nightfall and gathered only once a week for prayer and a shared meal. "They abandon their property without being influenced by any predominant attraction, they flee without even turning their heads back again,"[2] Philo marveled. The third-century church historian Eusebius was so impressed by their devotion, he was convinced they were actually early Christians.

What was the secret to their extreme piety? Philo offered an explanation. "Having first laid down self-control as a foundation for the soul," he wrote, "they build the other virtues on it."[3]

The line jumped off the page for me. *A foundation for the soul.* I found the paradox striking. A foundation is solid, immovable. A soul, by definition, is the opposite—airy and immaterial. Yet there they were, mashed together in one lovely phrase written millennia ago.

I was even more moved by the insight they conveyed. I didn't aspire to an ascetic life of punishing purity, but I recognized that these ancient monks were onto something. Self-control isn't just one good character trait, a nice addition to the pantheon of virtues. It's foundational. Not because it's more important than other virtues, but because the others rely upon it.

Think about it. Can you be faithful to your spouse without self-control? Can you be generous without self-control? Peaceable? Selfless? Honest? Kind? No, even the most basic altruism requires suspending your own interests to think of others. And that can't happen without self-control. The theologian Thomas Aquinas called temperance (another word for self-control) a cardinal virtue. He taught that none of the other virtues—including humility, meekness, mercy, and studiousness—could be developed without it.[4] As a statement from Fuller Seminary's Thrive Center puts it: "Self-control is an instrumental virtue. It facilitates the acquisition/development of other virtues: joy, gratitude, generosity."[5]

Self-control is key.

The insight about my lack of self-control was enlightening—and unsettling. I realized that lurking behind my inability to make progress was a deficiency in this cardinal virtue. My lack of spiritual progress wasn't a matter of adequate knowledge. I wasn't short on resources or strategies. I didn't lack time or opportunities or talent. The chief reason I couldn't follow through on my plans, why I felt chronically stuck in my spiritual life, why my best-laid plans and highest ambitions went unfulfilled day after day, year after year, really boiled down to one maddening, embarrassing, surprising, and undeniable truth: I lacked self-control. And making ancillary changes wasn't going to fix the problem. Sure, I could busy myself rearranging the furniture of my life. Add some cute shutters and a fresh coat of paint. But if things were really going to change, I had to work on the foundation.

The book you're holding is my attempt to do just that. Books are written by people who have either mastered a topic or by those who desperately need to. I fall into the latter camp. I'm going to explore the science and spirituality of self-control, research strategies for fostering this essential trait—then run experiments in the laboratory I call my life. While this is a personal journey, I don't plan to go it alone. I'll be talking with theologians and pastors, sociologists and psychologists. Self-control is a spiritual topic—and a psychological one. All truth is God's truth, and I'm scouting for wisdom wherever I can find it.

I'm not looking to become a multimillionaire, or release the giant within, or follow my bliss, or any other silly self-help fantasy. My hopes are more modest. I want to make progress in important areas of life by cultivating self-control. I want a firmer foundation for my soul.

If you have the same goal, keep reading . . .

Chapter 1

Why Self-Control?

Because It Leads to Freedom and Flourishing

"He who reigns within himself and rules passions, desires, and fears is more than a king."

—JOHN MILTON

Whenever you lose control, someone else always finds it."

These were the words of my high school English teacher Mr. Sologar on our first day of class. They didn't have anything to do with literature or grammar, but I guess he wanted to kick off the class with a life lesson.

It was a good one.

If we acted up at home, he explained, control of our lives would swiftly transfer to our parents in the form of lost privileges or being grounded. The same was true at school. If we abused our freedom in the classroom or in the hallways—and we did!—we'd find ourselves in the principal's office or confined to detention. If we got really crazy and decided to break the law, the legal system would step in to curtail our freedom.

"No, control is never truly lost," he repeated in his thick Indian accent. "If you fail to control yourself, others will control you."

I didn't care for Mr. Sologar. He covered our papers in red

The biggest threat to our freedom isn't any external enemy. It's our inability to control ourselves.

ink, hectored us about poor diction (he would have liked the word *hectored*), and insisted we read *The Lord of the Flies* even though there was a perfectly good movie based on the novel. Yet somehow his self-control lesson lodged itself in my lazy, teenage brain. There it sat, dormant and almost forgotten until I started researching for this book. Only now am I starting to truly appreciate the wisdom of his words. As he looked out across a class of adolescents, he knew the biggest threat to our freedom isn't any external enemy. It's our inability to control ourselves.

Mr. Sologar, you were onto something.

CONQUERING CITIES

The Bible has a lot to say about self-control. In that great repository of wisdom called Proverbs, we're told that it's "better to have self-control than to conquer a city" (Prov. 16:32 NLT). I'll admit that the city-conquering language feels a little weird to me (I'm more of a Cappuccino-conqueror), but I get the point. In the ancient world, people built massive walls around cities and patrolled them with armed guards. Conquering a city was the hardest military feat imaginable. But here's Solomon, the wisest guy in antiquity, saying that controlling yourself is more impressive than pulling off this nearly impossible exploit. The image also provides a telling contrast between two kinds of enemies. Defeating the enemy beyond your walls is hard; subduing the enemy within is harder.

Proverbs revisits the city-smashing motif elsewhere to hammer home the point. "Like a city whose walls are broken through is a person who lacks self-control" (Prov. 25:28). In other words, an absence of self-control is dangerous. Soldiers-breaking-through-your-walls dangerous.

It's not all wall breaking and city smashing. In one of the most beautiful passages in all of Scripture, the apostle Paul lists self-control alongside core virtues like love, joy, and peace as among the "fruit of the Spirit" (Gal. 5:22). We tend to think of self-control as a strictly human enterprise, but Scripture describes self-control as a product of being connected to God. It's something that grows when your life is rooted in divine reality. In fact, if it's missing, your faith may be a ruse. No fruit, no root.

These are just a few mentions of the virtue. Scripture is also crammed with examples of self-control in action, people who demonstrated this vital virtue as they served God and their fellow man.

The Bible portrays self-control not as restrictive but rather as the path to freedom. It enables us to do what's right—and ultimately what's best for us.

Unfortunately, self-control has a bad reputation these days. When I told people I was writing a book on the topic, I heard a lot of sighs and groans. "Oh yeah, I should be better about that," they would say, their voices tinged with defeat. Most of us view self-control like that overdue dentist appointment—necessary but dreaded. Others don't even see the necessity. The self doesn't need to be controlled; it needs to be liberated. For them, *self-expression* is the real virtue. Self-control is boring, confining, the cop that shows up and shuts down the party.

Others worry emphasizing self-control will lead to legalism, an approach to spiritual life that reduces faith to a list of dos and don'ts. Yet it's a mistake to relegate self-control to this category. Biblical self-control isn't about proud self-reliance or earning your way to heaven. It's not somehow nullified by grace. You will find no asterisks beside the biblical exhortations to exercise self-control. What you will find is a truckload of commands to resist evil, flee lust, avoid temptation, abstain from sin, control your tongue, guard your heart, and, most graphically, kill the flesh.

Yet these drastic measures aren't meant to confine us; they are edicts from a loving God designed to bring liberty. The Bible portrays self-control not as restrictive but rather as the path to freedom. It enables us to do what's right—and ultimately what's best for us.

From the biblical view, there are only two modes of life available to us: enslavement to sin and life in the Spirit. The former speaks of confinement in the extreme. Today "sin" is a playful word, associated with decadent desserts and lingerie ads. We see the word *sin* and imagine someone sampling a menu of forbidden delights. Don't be thrown by that connotation. Instead, think of being pistol-whipped by increasingly destructive patterns of behavior, ones that ultimately lead to your demise. That's what the Bible means by sin: enslavement. The early theologian Augustine (who knew a thing or two about sin) described it this way: "vanquished by the sin into which it fell by the bent of its will, nature has lost its liberty."[1]

Life in the Spirit, on the other hand, is a life of liberty. In this scenario a loving God guides and empowers you to live a life of righteousness that leads to flourishing and joy. But without self-control, you're doomed to the enslavement side of the equation.

RESISTING MARSHMALLOWS

For the past year, I've been reading everything about self-control I can get my hands on. Primarily that meant surveying the relevant Bible passages and diving into the vast corpus of Christian thought on the topic. I've also scoured academic journals and pored over dozens of studies. I've read bestselling books about grit and willpower and resilience and habits. I've interviewed experts in a variety of disciplines. Along the way, I've acquired a new vocabulary to talk about the subject. *Self-regulation. Ego depletion. Delayed gratification. Active volition. Inhibitory control.* All fancy ways of referring to our ability—or inability—to control our behavior.

It's been a fascinating journey, even if the material at times has been a little dry. Let's just say that studies with titles like "Cognitive, affective, and behavioral correlates of internalization of regulations for religious activities" aren't exactly beach reading. No matter. There have been enough revelations along the way to keep me going. More than once I've had my assumptions about self-control challenged—or flipped upside-down. Which is to be expected. Even those who study the subject for a living have been stunned by the discoveries of recent years.

One of the biggest surprises is just how powerful self-control is. Researchers first caught wind of the importance of self-control thanks to a 1960s experiment. In the now famous "marshmallow experiment," Stanford researcher Walter Mischel put a group of preschoolers through a wrenching test.[2] Each child was offered a marshmallow, cookie, or pretzel to eat. Or they could make a deal. The tikes were told that if they could hold off eating the sweet or salty treat for just fifteen minutes they would receive *two* treats.

Almost none of them could.

A few jammed the yummy snack into their mouths imme- diately. Most at least tried to resist. The children who held out employed a range of behaviors to cope with the temptation. Some would put their hands over their eyes or turn away from the tray bearing the delicious temptation. Out of sight, out of mind, they hoped. Others started kicking the desk or tugging on their hair. Some even played with the marshmallow, stroking it "as if it were a tiny stuffed animal."

The researchers analyzed the results, charting the children on a four-point scale on their ability to delay gratification. But the big findings wouldn't come until decades later and completely by chance. As fate would have it, Mischel's own daughters at- tended school with several children who had participated in the experiment. Over the years, he heard secondhand reports from his daughters about how their classmates were doing. Mischel noticed a pattern in the gossip. The children who seemed to get in the most trouble were the same ones who had trouble waiting for a second marshmallow.

His curiosity was piqued. Mischel and his colleagues tracked down hundreds of participants from the original study, now teen- agers. Sure enough, the ones who had demonstrated the higher levels of willpower as preschoolers were outpacing their peers. Not only did they have better grades and test scores, they were more popular at school and less likely to abuse drugs. The benefits continued to mount as the test subjects grew older. The children who had held out for the full fifteen minutes scored 210 points higher on their SATS than their weakest willed counterparts. They went on to achieve higher levels of education and report higher levels of happiness in their relationships. They even had lower body mass indexes.

Part of what made the follow-up findings so remarkable is that very few childhood traits are helpful in predicting outcomes later in life. Yet this simple test had shown a strong correlation between the ability to delay gratification in childhood with numerous benefits in adulthood.

If you could bottle self-control, it would be one of the most valuable substances on earth.

The findings rippled through multiple fields. Psychologists had long assumed intelligence was the key to a successful life. For educators, high self-esteem was the ticket. Self-control had never entered the discussion. But Mischel's marshmallow test changed everything. It showed that self-control was paramount and affected virtually every area of life. Since Mischel's famous experiment, study after study has linked self-control to a surplus of "favorable life outcomes," including better relationships, higher incomes, and higher levels of happiness. People with greater self-control are more sociable, honest, and sacrificial. They have lower rates of depression, anxiety, substance abuse, and aggression. They even live longer. If you could bottle self-control, it would be one of the most valuable substances on earth.

I'LL BE GOOD . . . LATER

Some researchers define self-control as the ability to delay gratification. This is what the marshmallow experiment sought to test. Can you resist the smaller immediate reward for a bigger one later? On paper, it looks like a no-brainer. The smart move is to hold out for the better reward. But desire has a way of changing the game, and not just for preschoolers. You know that passing on that donut now will make you feel healthier and more energetic tomorrow . . . but wait, is that a maple glaze?

Our inability to delay gratification lands us in all kinds of trouble. Perhaps the most famous example in the Bible involves a birthright and a bowl of soup. You might recall the story. The patriarch Isaac has twin sons, Jacob and Esau. Esau is born mere minutes before his brother, which means he's recognized as the firstborn. That might not seem like a big deal to us, but back then it was everything. The son with the birthright would eventually inherit all of the father's wealth and possessions.

The boys grow up, and they're complete opposites. Esau is a man's man. He excels at hunting and growing body hair (seriously . . . see Gen. 27:11). Jacob is a committed indoorsman who knows his way around the kitchen. One day Esau comes back from a hunt and he's starving. "Quick, let me have some of that red stew! I'm famished," he says to his brother. Jacob agrees to serve him the stew—on one condition. Esau has to give up his birthright. On the face of it, it's the most ludicrous offer of all time: one meal in exchange for a fortune. But Esau is hungry. And that makes all the difference. "Look, I am about to die," Esau says. "What good is the birthright to me?"

Esau was crazy, right? He was, but we all have a little Esau in us. We have a hard time holding out for future rewards, even when it's clearly in our best interest to do so. We tend to opt for the smaller, short-term payoff.

We whip out the credit card to buy things we don't need, knowing we'll have to pay it back later, plus interest.

We eat too much, knowing it will cause health problems down the road.

We indulge in sinful behaviors fully aware that doing so will damage our relationship with God and with others.

Somehow we lose sight of the bigger picture and grasp for the immediate pleasure. We eat the marshmallow. We trade for the soup. We take the easy way out. Self-control sounds like a lovely idea, but it's something we'll get to tomorrow. Augustine's prayer could be our own: "Grant me chastity and self-control, but please not yet."[3]

WHAT'S AT STAKE?

As I'm writing this chapter, the news is crammed with instances of high-profile moral failings. It seems every day brings new revelations of a Hollywood executive or politician accused of sexual assault or harassment. If the allegations are true—and most of them sure seem to be—it's hard to imagine what these people were thinking. Not only did their actions degrade and traumatize other people, they boomeranged back on them and destroyed their reputations and careers.

It's easy to dismiss these issues as secular problems. Many Christians experienced an acute sense of *schadenfreude* as we watched "godless" Hollywood consumed by the scandals. But sadly, the church has been home to similar behavior. For years, I edited a prominent ministry magazine, which brought me into close contact with many of the top church leaders in the country. I remember one up-and-coming leader I got to know. Charismatic and talented, he led a megachurch, headlined conferences around the country, and wrote bestselling books—and then lost it all when he was caught having extramarital affairs. I wish I could say his story was anomalous, but I lost count of how many leaders and friends torpedoed their ministries by succumbing to lust or greed.

In the midst of the scandals unfolding in 2017, theologian Owen Strachan took to social media to share this leadership lesson with his followers:

> Now more than ever, one moment can destroy—in one day—your life's work. The essential virtue: self-control. You can have all the talent in the world, and draw a ton of attention for it, but if your ability is not matched by strong character, you are in a precarious place.[4]

As Strachan observed, a lack of self-control has dire consequences. And it's not just politicians and pastors who need to heed his warning. For all of us, even a momentary break in willpower can cause irreversible damage. Yet preventing these kinds of dramatic failings is just one function of self-control. It also plays a central role in the thousands of small decisions we face every day.

A lack of self-control has dire consequences. And it's not just politicians and pastors who need to heed his warning. For all of us, even a momentary break in willpower can cause irreversible damage.

Social scientists define self-control as the ability to resist negative impulses. But when the Bible mentions self-control, it usually has something bigger in mind. Yes, it involves the ability to resist doing something you shouldn't. But it also has a proactive element. It refers to the ability to do something you should. In theological terms, it's about guarding against sins of commission (bad things you do) and sins of omission (good things you fail to do). It also involves resisting the entire range of unwelcome impulses: from the instinct to eat that second piece of chocolate cake to the temptation to look at pornography.

When you think of self-control in these terms, you see how it impacts every facet of life. Just think of an average day. It starts before you even open your eyes. Your alarm goes off and you're faced with a decision. Grab some extra sleep or use the extra minutes doing something useful. Sometimes it's fine to grab the extra Zs (you probably need them). But usually you're better off using those precious before-the-craziness-of-the-day moments to spend some time with God or get some exercise. So do you linger in bed or do something productive? Depends on self-control.

Next comes breakfast. Do you grab a donut and coffee on the way out the door? Or opt for a healthier option, which, in addition to not tasting as good, likely takes more time to prepare? Again, self-control.

On the way to work, you get cut off. Then you hit gridlock traffic. Another decision: lose your cool and cuss, or take a deep breath and let the incident roll off your back? More self-control.

At work you face a jungle of dilemmas. Do you spend the first hour at your desk surfing the web? Or dive straight in and make some progress on that important report? When people start gossiping about that annoying coworker, do you join in or defend him? When you notice that someone seems discouraged, do you risk a little awkwardness by walking into their office and showing concern? Or do you just ignore it and stick to your routine? Do you gripe about the boss? Do you look a little too long at that attractive coworker?

It's all self-control.

When you return home, the challenges continue. And now you're tired, making self-control even harder. Do you just melt into the couch and let the cable TV wash over you? Or do you spend some quality time with your kids? Do you eat too much at dinner? Or drink too much after it? Do you spend the meal staring at your phone or conversing with your family? After the kids go to bed, do you watch Netflix or take the opportunity to spend some meaningful time with your spouse and deepen your marriage?

It's not just 9–5 workers who face such choices. They come at every stage of life. If you're a stay-at-home parent, do you park the kids in front of the TV? Or do you lead them in constructive activities that demand more of your attention? Do you routinely feed your children sugary snacks or push nutritional meals (even when they act like you're torturing them)? If you're a retiree, do you live for your personal hobbies or pour into members of the next generation? If you're a college student, do you start on that essay early in the semester or cram the day before it's due? Do you Snapchat with friends during class or listen to the lectures?

There are times where it's perfectly okay to just veg out. We need down time. But too often we choose the easier, and sometimes sinful, option rather than doing things that would ultimately enrich our lives, help others, and foster growth. And typically, the difference doesn't amount to ignorance of what choice is better; it's usually a matter of self-control.

While we may be tested in dramatic moments, the fabric of life is stitched slowly, through a thousand tiny choices that end up defining your life.

It's easy to imagine your life's

28

outcome as the product of a few big decisions. We envision a lone hero showing extraordinary courage at a climactic moment. Or a tragic figure losing control at a critical juncture. That might be how things work in the movies.

In reality, our destinies are determined in a more mundane manner. As the writer Annie Dillard reminds us, "How we spend our days is, of course, how we spend our lives."[5] While we may be tested in dramatic moments, the fabric of life is stitched slowly, through a thousand tiny choices that end up defining our lives. The difference of those accumulated decisions is dramatic. They can add up to a life crippled by sloth and sin or to one character- ized by freedom and flourishing.

THE GYMNAST CONFRONTS HER ABUSER

Among all the public sex scandals in recent years, none was more disturbing than the case involving Larry Nasser, the former Team USA gymnastics doctor who was accused of molesting 250 young women. The first to draw attention to Nasser's sexual abuse was Rachael Denhollander, a former gymnast the doctor abused. At Nasser's sentencing, Denhol- lander addressed him for forty minutes. Drawing from her Christian faith, she spoke of God's judgment and mercy.

"The Bible you speak carries a final judgment where all of God's wrath and eternal terror is poured out on men like you. Should you ever reach the point of truly facing what you have done, the guilt will be crushing. And that is what makes the gospel of Christ so sweet. Because it extends grace and hope and mercy where none should be found. And it will be there for you."[6]

In her address, Denhollander also confronted Nasser about his selfishness and lack of self-control.

"You have become a man ruled by selfish and perverted desires, a man defined by his daily choices repeatedly to feed that selfishness and perversion. You chose to pursue your wickedness no matter what it cost others and the opposite of what you have done is for me to choose to love sacrificially, no matter what it costs me."[7]

TERMS OF SURRENDER

Okay, so self-control is important. But what exactly is it?

As we've seen, the ability to delay gratification is crucial. But there's more to self-control than postponing pleasure. In some situations we're not sure if doing the right thing will result in a bigger reward down the road. Yet exercising self-control demands doing the right thing anyway. For a more comprehensive understanding of this essential character trait we must look to Scripture.

The New Testament uses four words that we translate as self-control. Each highlights a different aspect of the virtue. If you'll indulge me, I'm going to dust off my seminary Greek and take a brief look at each one. (I promise to keep it short and sweet.)

Néphō literally means "to be sober, to abstain from wine." It is also used figuratively, to speak of being free from the intoxicating effects of sin. *Néphō* is used in passages that warn against being duped by false teachers (2 Tim. 4:5) and becoming prey for the devil's attacks (1 Peter 5:8). It stresses the need for clear-eyed vigilance. *Nḗphō* describes a crucial precondition to resisting temptation. We need clear vision to spot sin and avoid it.

Chalinagógeó (don't you love these Greek words?!) means "to bridle or restrain." The word invokes the image of a horse controlled and directed by a mouth bit. James uses the word to describe the formidable task of taming the tongue (James 1:26) and controlling the body (3:2). Like a large animal, our sinful desires are powerful. Self-control demands we direct and restrain them.

Sṓphrōn describes someone with a "sound mind" who is "balanced." According to Scripture, it is especially important for elderly men and church leaders to possess this key attribute (1 Tim. 3:2; Titus 2:2). Though *sṓphrōn* denotes moderation, it doesn't speak of a safe, middle-of-the-road mentality. Rather it portrays a mindset that is righteous and therefore temperate. The person who has this quality is not prone to erratic, impulsive behavior.

Egkráteia translates as "self-mastery" or literally "dominion within." The most familiar usage of this word comes in Galatians 5, where Paul lists *egkráteia* alongside the other fruit of the Spirit. People who exhibit this quality are not mastered by their passions. They have internal control.

You can probably see how these Greek words relate to our understanding of self-control—and how they expand on it. The biblical concept of self-control goes far beyond the mere ability to hold out for future rewards. These concepts describe mentalities and habits and character traits. Someone who embodies these virtues is sober and restrained, balanced and mastered.

When I look at that list, I'm both impressed and intimidated. I don't know about you, but I wouldn't use those words to describe myself. Not all the time, anyway. Don't get me wrong. I want to cultivate those attributes (that's why I've tackled this project after all), but doing so is a daunting prospect. It requires more than curbing a bad habit or two; it demands growth in multiple core areas. And growth is painful.

But here's the good news. When it comes to developing self-control, we're not expected to go at it alone. Thank God for that! As we walk closely with Him, He promises to guide and empower us. We tend to think of self-control as an independent virtue. After all, we're talking about *self*-control. Isn't it primarily about us? I would argue, no.

What self-control requires, ultimately, isn't control but surrender.

As we'll discuss later, there is certainly a role for human effort. But there's a giant paradox at the heart of this issue. What self-control requires, ultimately, isn't control but surrender.

Above I defined *egkráteia* as "self-mastery." If any virtue would be dependent on me, it seems like this would be it. "Self-mastery" makes me think of someone with ninja-level discipline, completely self-sufficient. Yet Scripture is clear that this self-mastery isn't an attribute that can be developed apart from God. Remember, Paul calls it a "fruit of the Spirit." He's invoking a metaphor. Just like a tree must be nourished by the soil to produce fruit, so we must be connected to God in order to see this virtue flourish in our lives. As a result, *egkráteia*, as one commentator states, "can only be accomplished *by the power of the Lord*."[8] There's a similar dynamic with *sōphrōn*. As another commentator puts it, the word describes someone "who does not command himself, but rather is commanded by God."[9] Ultimately, mastering yourself is only accomplished by being mastered by God.

Self-control implies a struggle. We're conflicted creatures, beset by sinful desires and selfish impulses. Part of us wants to do the right thing. Another part wants to do what's easy or most pleasurable. Stanford psychologist Kelly McGonigal provides a definition of self-control that gets to the heart of this reality. She defines self-control as "the ability to do what you need to do, even if part of you doesn't want to."[10] My definition is even shorter. *Self-control is the ability to do the right thing, even when you don't feel like it.*

Sounds simple enough. But for Christians, there's a catch. We believe that "the right thing" to do has been determined by God. He knows what's best for us. He's shown us what's right and wrong through His Word, and He speaks to us through the quiet witness of our conscience. Self-control, then, is about listening and obeying. It's not self-determined. It means submitting every decision we make to God. It's about surrendering. When we do this consistently, it's called self-control.

I realize this sounds hard. Delaying gratification, doing what's right, surrendering your will. It might seem like teeth-gritting, white-knuckling stuff. But it isn't. As we'll discover, though building self-control requires effort, it gets easier as you go. Eventually, it can feel like gliding. In a beautiful twist of biblical irony, submission leads to victory. Surrender produces freedom. As you are liberated from the tyranny of self, you're able to experience God's best for your life.

Next we're going to consider the role that purpose plays in developing self-control. Then we're going to look at the obstacles we face in developing this key virtue. It's going to get a little dark, but stick with me. There's a lot at stake. Your future self will thank you.

Self-Control Training:
Entry #1—The Mission

I WARNED YOU IN THE INTRODUCTION that this book was more than a theoretical exploration of the topic. In addition to investigating the spirituality and science of self-control, I said I was going to test out the ideas I encountered in my own life. And that's precisely what I plan to do.

But before I can jump into discussing specific strategies for improving my self-control, I need to understand what I'm up against. That will mean reckoning with my fallen nature and understanding how willpower works, which I'll do in the subsequent chapters. And before I can apply the wisdom of Scripture and the findings from social science, I feel like I need to identify the areas in my life where I need to grow.

How can I identify those areas of weakness? I suppose I could try to take a hard look at my life and be brutally honest with myself. The problem is that self-assessment is notoriously unreliable. Have you ever lamented a personal shortcoming only to have someone look at you with confusion and say, "Actually, I think you're really strong in that area"? Try as we might, we don't always see ourselves clearly. An outsider perspective does wonders for alerting us to our faults.

So I decided I needed some outside help. But from whom? It would have to be someone who knew me well and cared about me, who was kind. I also needed someone tough. This job required a person who would be honest enough to cut through my nonsense and talk to me straight about my battle with self-control. Hmm . . .

"Honey, can you help me out with something?"

Chapter 2

Sorry, Self-Control Isn't about You

How the Right Purpose Guides and Fuels Self-Control

He who has a "why" to live for can bear almost any "how."

—FRIEDRICH NIETZSCHE

I keep circling back to a problem. In the introduction I mentioned how I felt frustrated, stuck. I expected to make more progress in my life, but I wasn't seeing it. Eventually I came to the realization that improving my self-control was the key to making headway. But here's the rub. I know that Christianity isn't a success course. It's not a self-improvement program. In fact, it's not really about me. Not primarily anyway. The end goal for a Christian isn't to become such an impressive, successful person that you can stand atop a mountain of accomplishments and declare, "Look at me!"

Let's say that I could harness the discipline necessary to become successful and rich and get in perfect shape. I know I'd be impressed, so impressed I'd injure my shoulder patting myself on the back. Maybe you'd be impressed, too. But would God? Not likely.

In fact, all throughout Scripture, God seems to make a point of using nobodies to accomplish His purposes. After all, it wasn't the elite who hung out with Jesus; it was the prostitutes and tax collectors. God seems to take pleasure in subverting the hierarchies of the world. In God's economy, servants are the leaders, the meek inherit the earth, the poor are blessed, enemies are loved, the humble are exalted, the foolish things shame the wise, those who seek their lives lose them, and those who finish last hoist the first place trophy. You get the picture. In this upside-down kingdom, what role does self-control play? Ultimately, what is it *for*?

DRIVEN—AND DERAILED

There's something even scarier to me than an absence of self-control: developing self-control for the wrong reasons. I'd hate to acquire the discipline required to reach my goals only to realize too late that I'd chosen the wrong ones or pursued them for the wrong reasons. As the monk Thomas Merton wrote, "People may spend their whole lives climbing the ladder of success only to find, once they reach the top, that the ladder is leaning against the wrong wall." That's why, in addition to discussing *how* to develop self-control, we must determine *why*. Before you start scaling the ladder, you have to find the right wall. And the right wall is not ourselves. Enough people have leaned their ladder against that flimsy façade, scaled to the top, and came crashing down hard.

I read a powerful story from business thinker Clayton M. Christensen that drove home this point for me. Christensen, who graduated from the prestigious Harvard Business School (HBS), writes about how he's witnessed talented and hard-working colleagues ruin their lives:

> Over the years I've watched the fates of my HBS classmates from 1979 unfold; I've seen more and more of them come to reunions unhappy, divorced, and alienated from their children. I can guarantee you that not a single one of them graduate with the deliberate strategy of getting divorced and raising children who would become estranged from them. And yet a shocking number of them implemented that strategy.[1]

What went wrong with these promising HBS grads? According to Christensen, it boiled down to a strategic error: "They didn't keep the purpose of their lives front and center as they decided how to spend their time, talents, and energy."[2]

Christensen believes he was rescued from similar heartache by a practice he instituted while he was a student at Oxford: "I decided to spend an hour every night reading, thinking, and praying about why God put me on this earth." But many of his peers never established a worthwhile purpose and ended up sabotaging themselves. "People who are driven to excel have this unconscious propensity to underinvest in their families and overinvest in their careers," he writes. They "inadvertently invested for lives of hollow unhappiness."[3]

What makes the plight of these HBS grads so sobering is that they're the last people you would expect to lead "lives of hollow unhappiness." Intelligent, educated, and hard-working, they had every opportunity in life. The problem was they had no ultimate purpose, so their priorities were skewed. They ended up living for themselves, which meant pursuing career at the expense of relationships. It's a cautionary story worth heeding. They served themselves and they ended up alone.

They ended up living for themselves, which meant pursuing career at the expense of relationships. They served themselves and they ended up alone.

Unfortunately, much of the material on self-control simply perpetuates this problem. Recently at the local bookstore, I surveyed the literature on developing discipline and was struck by how often words like "Power" and "Success" appeared in the titles. Self-control is presented as a means to get rich or popular or wealthy. It encourages people to set goals—whatever goals they want—and pursue them with single-minded determination. But biblical self-control can't be divorced from biblical purposes. And we know what those purposes are.

When Jesus was asked, "Which is the greatest commandment?," His reply was simple: "'Love the Lord your God with all your heart and with all your soul and with all your mind.' This is the first and greatest commandment." Then He added this addendum: "And the second is like it: 'Love your neighbor as yourself.' All the Law and the Prophets hang on these two commandments" (Matt. 22:36–40).

The religious leader who posed the commandment question had sinister motives. He was "testing" Jesus, trying to trip Him up and discredit Him. But thanks to his question, we have a perfect distillation of God's law, right from the mouth of God's Son. Call it the divinely inspired purpose statement. If you really want to bottom-line things, if you truly desire to know what's most important, here's what you need to do:

Love God. Love others.

Unfortunately, we don't always obey those commands. Why? Because our hearts are all messed up.

OUT OF ORDER

The fourth-century theologian Augustine knew a lot about sin. He's the one who uttered the highly questionable prayer: "Grant me chastity and self-control, but please not yet."[4] Even as he cried out for freedom from sin, he could still feel its pull.

Ultimately, though, Augustine concluded that sin wasn't merely about individual acts. It was about the heart. He believed that what you love is the most important thing about who you are. But he observed that we tend to have "disordered loves." In other words, we love some things more than we should. And we love other things less than we should. We should love people more than possessions, but often our hearts prize the latter more than the former. We should desire God more than His gifts, but we get that mixed up too.

These disordered loves cause all kinds of problems. Pastor Tim Keller offers this example. "There is nothing wrong with loving your work, but if you love it more than your family, then your loves are out of order and you may ruin your family."[5] When I read that example, I couldn't help think of Christensen's colleagues: their personal lives were destroyed by disordered loves.

Loving career more than family is just one example of disordered love. From a Christian perspective, not even family should command our highest devotion. That spot is reserved for your

Creator. Keller explains: "The ultimate disordered love, however —and the ultimate source of our discontent—is failure to love *the* first thing first, the failure to love God supremely."[6] There's a cruel irony that comes into play whenever we value something above God. If we prioritize happiness above all else, we will never find happiness. If we grant marriage or family or work the highest place in our hearts, we will end up hurting those too. These are all good things, but they were never meant to bear the full weight of our ultimate allegiance.

Lavishing our highest love on something other than God leaves us empty, dissatisfied. We have a "God-shaped vacuum" in our hearts. Only when we grant God our highest love do we find the contentment we crave. As Augustine wrote, "You have made us for yourself, and our heart is restless until it rests in you."[7]

Biblical self-control is about keeping our loves in the right order. In a sense, we can only do what we love. When we succumb to sin, it's because in that moment, we loved something else—pleasure, pride, comfort—more than God. We will always operate out of our loves. That means we must rightly order our hearts, taking special care to ensure we are not worshiping anything or anyone other than God. Doing so will also help us fulfill the second greatest commandment: loving others.

Loving others doesn't come naturally for us. We're selfish creatures; we tend to put our needs and interests first. The needs of others? We'll get to them . . . if there's enough time. It takes discipline to resist this selfish impulse and serve others. It's hardly a natural thing to do.

People often comment on what a "natural mother" my wife, Grace, is. Indeed, she's an excellent mom. After working full-time for the first eight years of our marriage, she now spends her days at home with our three young children. I marvel at her ability to read children's books (over and over), do kids' crafts, play toys with them, clean up spills, and otherwise entertain, discipline, educate, correct, and comfort little human beings. But she'll be the first one to tell you that these activities don't come naturally for her. Some people enjoy the trappings of childcare. Interacting with small children and entering their world energizes them. Not her. Before we had children, Grace would volunteer in the church nursery and come out frazzled. When she was a teenager, she found babysitting stressful. Even caring for our children has been challenging. "I don't love playing kids' games and reading kids' books," she told me. "But I love our kids so much that I'm happy to do those things." Grace isn't a hero; she's a mom. And because she loves her children she consistently puts her own preferences aside. She exercises self-control to do what's best for them.

The same principle applies when it comes to loving people outside our biological family. It's no coincidence that the fruit of the Spirit Paul lists (love, joy, peace, patience, kindness, goodness, faithfulness, gentleness, and self-control) has a communal dimension. In fact, most aren't virtues per se. They're more like states of being designed to promote interpersonal harmony. By placing self-control at the end of this list, I believe Paul is emphasizing its value for relationships. Being self-controlled enables us to suspend our interests enough to truly love others. As Sir Alec Paterson prayed, "O God, help us to be masters of ourselves that we may be servants of others."[8]

Once you understand self-control in this way, the very idea of using it for selfish reasons becomes a contradiction, an absurdity. The first job of self-control is resisting the temptation to put yourself first. There's a certain pain in loosening your grip on self-centeredness. Like Augustine, you feel like crying out for God to free you from the slavery of sin—but please not yet.

Ultimately, self-control isn't about you. It's about surrendering to God's purposes for you. And it's not about getting success or money or power. In the end, it's about love.

Of course loving God and others ends up being the best thing for you. Paradoxically, that's how you discover true joy and fulfillment. But you can't do it by placing yourself on the throne of your own heart. You will indeed find your life, but only once you're willing to lose it. Once you surrender, however, the true adventure begins. Self-control becomes a powerful tool for living a life that glorifies God and blesses others. Ultimately, self-control isn't about you. It's about surrendering to God's purposes for you. And it's not about getting success or money or power. In the end, it's about love.

PURPOSE IS AN ENGINE

We know a lot today about the mechanics of self-control. Thanks to an explosion of research from social scientists over the past two decades, we have a greater understanding of the subject than ever before. We know how willpower works, why it fails, and what we can do to rein in our impulses. We can map out the areas of the brain involved in resisting temptation and overcoming challenges. We also have a host of tools and tactics to help us change our behavior. These insights and strategies are valuable, and we'll explore them in this book. Yet as we survey strategies for increasing willpower and improving "self-regulation," we can't forget the purpose of self-control. Loving God and others is our ultimate aim. But there's also a practical benefit to defining our ultimate purpose. Fo-

We can't forget the purpose of self-control. Loving God and others is our ultimate aim.

cusing on a transcendent goal actually fuels the formation of self-control. Purpose is like a steering wheel and an engine. It guides and propels us.

The life of Paul provides a perfect example. While Paul lamented his struggles with self-control, it's apparent he was no slacker. Consider just a few of the things he accomplished. He evangelized huge swaths of the Roman Empire (on foot!), wrote almost a third of the New Testament (often from jail!), and nurtured church plants across the empire. And he did so all in the teeth of violent opposition. At one point, Paul provides a sample of the hardships he endured along the way: shipwrecks, lashings, imprisonment, a stoning, hunger, nakedness, sleeplessness, and constant danger. On top of all that, he adds, "I face the daily pressure of my concern for all the churches" (2 Cor. 11:28).

How could Paul withstand these hardships and keep going? I'm guessing most people would have given up after just a sampling of the persecution he experienced. Take, for instance, the lashings he received. This was a customary Roman punishment for criminals. The offender was given forty lashes, minus one. That's thirty-nine strokes on the back with a whip that was cruelly outfitted with small pieces of bone and metal designed to rip away chunks of flesh. I think one of these sessions would probably be enough to stop me. Paul endured five.

Why did Paul do it?

Fortunately, we don't have to speculate about his motives, because he came right out and told us what they were. "Forgetting what is behind and straining toward what is ahead, I press on toward the goal to win the prize for which God has called me heavenward in Christ Jesus" (Phil. 3:13–14).

Paul's extraordinary feats weren't undertaken to impress onlookers. He wasn't interested in flaunting his steely resolve or pursuing selfish ends. It wasn't self-control for self-control's sake. He did it for an ultimate purpose: to win the "prize" of being united to Christ and to help as many people as possible do the same. That's what kept him going. That's the bright future he glimpsed as he languished in dark prisons. That's the comfort he felt as whips tore into his flesh. That's what fueled his determination and confidence. It's what gave him the *oomph* to stagger to his feet for the thousandth time and strike off for the next city. Paul had a purpose.

When Paul wrote to the Corinthians, urging them to live disciplined lives of self-control, he emphasized the necessity of keeping this ultimate purpose in sight. Comparing the Christian journey to a race, he asked, "Do you not know that in a race all the runners run, but only one gets the prize?" (1 Cor. 9:24).

The Corinthians were very familiar with races. Corinth was home to the Isthmian Games, a massive sporting event held every three years. It was second in popularity only to the Olympic Games held in Athens. Paul's words would have called to mind fresh images of athletes in the stadium, circling the hard-packed dirt track, their heads down and arms pumping. Paul points out what the Corinthians already knew. The runners weren't out there for the fresh air; they wanted to win. The purpose of the race was the prize.

But as Paul stresses, the key to winning prizes is preparation. "Everyone who competes in the games goes into strict training," he wrote (1 Cor. 9:25). We know from history just how strict the training for these Greek athletes was. Competitors in the Isthmian Games were required to provide proof that they had trained for at least ten months and were confined to the gymnasium for the thirty days preceding the games. When it came time to compete, some athletes pushed themselves so hard, they died.

Paul noted the impressive commitment of these athletes, and urged the Corinthians to have the same unwavering focus and discipline when it came to their spiritual journey. "Run in such a way as to get the prize," he implored (v. 24). And he reminded them that there was a crucial difference between the spiritual race and a physical one. While runners expended all their efforts "to get a crown that will not last," believers "do it to get a crown that will last forever" (v. 25). The winners in the Isthmian games received a wreath made from celery or pine leaves. Talk about temporary! The Corinthian believers were working for a reward that would last forever.

Having assured them of the reward, Paul gives a glimpse of his training regimen.

> Therefore I do not run like someone running aimlessly; I do not fight like a boxer beating the air. No, I strike a blow to my body and make it my slave so that after I have preached to others, I myself will not be disqualified for the prize. (1 Cor. 9:26–27)

That's strong language. Paul switches the analogy from racing to boxing and describes himself squaring off against his own fleshly desires. The words "strike a blow to my body" is translated from a Greek word that means "to give a black eye to." This doesn't mean that Paul literally hit his body. He forcibly subdued his sinful desires that threatened to make him forfeit the prize. But the flesh never goes down easy. It's a violent, sweaty struggle. Here we see an example of self-control as the "fierce fruit" of the Spirit in action.[9] Paul transforms his body from an enemy into an ally. He makes it his slave, an agent to serve his ultimate purpose rather than sabotaging it. Whereas before it threatened to take him out of the race, now it can help him win it.

I've been going to church all my life and can honestly say I've never heard a sermon with that kind of language. It seems we're reluctant to speak of the war against the flesh in the same graphic terms. Even when we do broach the topic of sin, we use language that implies a sort of helplessness and resignation. We "deal with" issues or "struggle with" sins. Rarely do we speak of defeating them. Seldom do we don the armor of God and fight. Perhaps it's no surprise then, that when temptation comes, we roll over for it. We shrug our shoulders and repeat some cliché about how no one is perfect.

We desperately need the kind of Spirit-empowered, sin-killing approach Paul described. And that comes only when we're focused on the prize. When Paul wrote these words, the church in Corinth was a mess. They were plagued with divisions. They were getting drunk at the Lord's Supper. One guy was sleeping with his father's wife. On top of it all, they were arrogant. Paul addressed these sinful behaviors, but ultimately to help them develop the self-control they so badly needed, he directed their eyes heavenward. He reminded them of their ultimate purpose. Like athletes, they must fight idleness and submit to training.

When I read this passage, I picture Paul as a track coach. It's like he's jogging alongside his spiritual trainees, shouting encouragements. "Have you heard about the prize? Don't you want to win? Run! Run! Run!" All the effort and sacrifice would be worth it, he assured them. No cost was too great to win the prize.

In some ways, Paul's advice to the Corinthians doesn't seem very practical. Was it really best to encourage them to think about heaven when they had so many problems right here on earth? Had I been in Paul's position, I might have handled things differently. I would have been more practical. "Let's get some guidelines in place to deal with your appalling lack of self-control," I would have said. "The Sunday school lesson on heaven can wait for later. Forget winning races; you just need to get back on your feet."

But Paul was right to direct their gaze heavenward. He knew that seeing the prize would help them run the race. That ultimate goal would infuse their efforts with meaning and help them push a little harder to overcome obstacles. It would equip them to endure.

SANCTIFIED GOALS

In 2009, University of Miami researchers Michael McCullough and Brian Willoughby did something weird. Well, at least it seemed weird to their fellow academics. They published a paper on the link between religion and self-control. "For a long time it wasn't cool for social scientists to study religion," McCullough explained. But when they started looking, they found "some researchers were quietly chugging along for decades."[10] McCullough and Willoughby examined these studies, and found "remarkably consistent findings that religiosity correlates with higher self-control."[11]

The studies went back nearly a hundred years. One from the 1920s found that children who went to Sunday school scored higher on tests measuring their self-discipline. McCullough and Willoughby also analyzed a dozen other studies showing that religious beliefs and practices boosted self-discipline, and not just for Sunday school kids. The positive impact cut across all age groups and socioeconomic strata, from "adolescents, university students, community-dwelling adults, and convicted drug offenders."[12]

So *how* did religion increase self-control?

Some of the explanations were hardly surprising. McCullough and Willoughby cited the influence of religious practices and rituals. Anyone who has sat through a long sermon on a hard pew understands the character-building value of such experiences. Then there was the benefit of having behavioral guidelines and accountability. But there was something more: what researchers call "sanctified goals," the tendency of believers to give spiritual significance to their endeavors. According to McCullough and Willoughby, this dynamic was powerful. "Goal sanctification of this nature appears to energize goal striving and, possibly, influence successful goal attainment."[13]

One self-identified "heathen," writing in *The New York Times*, was so impressed with McCullough's and Willoughby's findings he wondered, "If I'm serious about keeping my New Year's resolutions. . . . should the to-do list include, 'Start going to church'?" But McCullough burst his bubble, explaining to him that only true believers reap the benefits. "Religious people are self-controlled . . . because they've absorbed the ideals of their religion into their own system of values, and have thereby given their personal goals an aura of sacredness," McCullough told him. "The belief that God has preferences for how you behave and the goals you set for yourself has to be the granddaddy of all psychological devices for encouraging people to follow through with their goals."

It turns out that this "granddaddy of all psychological devices" exerts influence on just about every area of life. Studies show that couples who view their marriages as "manifestations of God" have better relationships and do better at resolving conflict. People who view their bodies as a "gift[s] from God" have healthier lifestyles. Workers who see their careers as a calling work harder and perform better at their jobs. It turns out that seeing your life through a spiritual lens has massive practical benefits.

To get a better understanding of this phenomenon, I talked to Sarah Schnitker, a professor of psychology at Baylor University who studies virtue and character development. Schnitker isn't surprised that religion boosts self-control. Though she's a psychologist, she's quick to point out that character building has religious roots. "Virtue formation historically wasn't the domain of psychology, because we didn't have psychology until modern times," she told me. "It was done in the context of the church. And it had an overarching purpose. It was about honoring God, benefiting community."

"Virtue formation . . . . was about honoring God, benefiting community."

Schnitker speculates that many attempts at developing character suffer by neglecting this heritage. "Secular efforts to build self-control have been ineffective because they don't have the spiritual telos [purpose]," she said. "When people are pursuing sanctified goals," she concluded, "they pursue them differently."

But why exactly do people pursue sanctified goals more effectively?

Schnitker pointed out one reason that seems pretty obvious, what I call the "God-is-always-watching" factor. "Beliefs about God affect the way people perform on self-control tests," Schnitker said. "If you believe in an omniscient, watchful God, you perform much better on temptation-resistance tests."

However, the power of sanctified goals isn't all due to the watchful eye in the sky. "Sanctification of even mundane goals changes the way people engage in goal pursuit," Schnitker explained. "So take a goal, say being a good parent. It's not necessarily a spiritual goal, but if you imbue that goal with sacred meaning, and say that God cares about this calling, you pursue goals related to that role with more effort." That's a benefit you don't get if you are motivated by more self-focused concerns. "We find that when you pursue happiness for your own sake, it often doesn't end well," Schnitker said. "You need another reason for why you're developing character."

Sanctified goals are actually easier to pursue. I talked to Elliot Berkman, a University of Oregon psychologist who specializes in the study of goals and motivation. "There's a deep connection between identity and motivation," he said. "A behavior that holds greater subjective value for a person will be relatively easy for them to complete versus tasks of lesser significance. These identity-linked goals are more likely to be successful."

In other words, we have an easier time pursuing goals when we believe they have an ultimate purpose, one that is closely aligned with our identity. That makes sense to me. I've known a lot of people who see their job as a calling, something with significance beyond earning a paycheck. They're the same people who report that their work doesn't feel like work. Sure, it can still be difficult. But because they believe it's important, it doesn't feel like a grind—and that belief in what they're doing keeps them motivated and focused.

I was intrigued by the idea of sanctified goals. I was convinced that seeing goals through a spiritual lens was thoroughly biblical. As Christians, all of our pursuits should ultimately be for God's glory—and no activity is too small or insignificant. As we're commanded in Colossians 3:23, "Whatever you do, work at it with all your heart, as working for the Lord, not for human masters." Furthermore, as the studies show, there are enormous practical benefits to having sanctified goals.

All too often I miss out on those benefits. I fail to consider what I'm doing through a spiritual lens. It's not that I pursue bad goals; I just have a tendency to leave God out of it. I go to church on Sunday, maybe even attend a prayer meeting or Bible study during the week—and then go back to living my "regular" life. Rarely do I pause to reflect on how everything I do—from attending meetings to returning emails to teaching my daughter how to ride a bike—connects to spiritual reality.

Rarely do I pause to reflect on how everything I do connects to spiritual reality.

It's a little frightening to consider how good I am at compartmentalizing life into sacred and secular categories. I'm starting to realize this is a dangerous dichotomy. If I'm not careful, I can live as a functional atheist, blind to the supernatural light illuminating the world. I need to train my imagination to see the eternal dimensions of my everyday life.

Not only is training our imagination to focus on our ultimate purpose thoroughly biblical, it will also strengthen our willpower and fortify our resolve. It will give us the passion we need to press on when things get tough. It will equip us to resist the temptations that threaten to distract and derail us along the way.

Doing that successfully will mean listening to the sweeter song. Let me explain.

TWO WAYS TO TACKLE TEMPTATION

In Homer's classic tale *The Odyssey*, the hero Odysseus embarks on a perilous journey. He must escape many dangers on his long voyage home from the Trojan War. None of these dangers is more deadly than the Sirens. These mythical mermaids are beautiful, seductive. But their appeal is deceptive. In truth, they're murderous creatures that use their sweet singing to lure sailors to their deaths.

Odysseus understands the danger. He knows he's vulnerable to their song. So he hatches a plan to sail past the Sirens without succumbing. He instructs his sailors to lash him to the mast of the ship. That way, even if Odysseus surrenders to the Sirens' song, he will be unable to free himself and go to them. He commands his sailors not to loosen the ropes, no matter how much he pleads with them to do so. They must ignore him and continue sailing. To make sure the sailors aren't seduced, Odysseus has them stuff their ears with beeswax so they won't hear the Sirens' singing.

The plan works. As Odysseus suspects, when he hears the Sirens, he's overcome with temptation. He tries to escape and pleads with the sailors to release him. But his sailors tighten the ropes and continue to sail.

This classic story provides us with one rather shrewd approach to temptation. Odysseus is wise to account for his weakness. He sees the danger coming and prepares. His precautions are extreme, but effective.

Many of the strategies in this book have an Odysseus flavor. They're about avoiding temptation and taking practical precautions to help guard against the flesh. They involve taking a realistic look at our nature and planning accordingly. We're wise to employ this strategy. Being aware of our sinful nature, preserving willpower, and building holy habits are critical. Only fools assume they can tough it out on their own.

But there's a second approach to temptation. It's different from Odysseus's plan and even more crucial to developing true self-control. This approach is depicted in the *Argonautica*, another Greek epic.

In this story, the Argonauts must sail past the same Sirens that threatened the sailors in *The Odyssey*. But they escape their deadly snare with a very different strategy. As they sail past the Sirens, they hear the singing. But they have the legendary musician and poet Orpheus on board. He draws his lyre and plays a louder and more beautiful song, drowning out the Sirens' music. Enthralled with Orpheus's "sweeter song," the sailors pass by in safety.

Ultimately the best way to avoid sin, the most powerful means of self-control, comes by listening to a "sweeter song."

It's an effective strategy, one that doesn't rely on ropes and beeswax. Instead of merely restraining the hand, it aims to capture the heart.

Like I said, there's nothing wrong with employing practical tools to avoid temptation. It's wise to anticipate temptations and take proactive steps to avoid giving in. Sometimes we have to lash ourselves to the mast. Tighten the ropes and keep sailing.

But ultimately the best way to avoid sin, the most powerful

means of self-control, comes by listening to a "sweeter song." For Christians, this means tuning in to God's ultimate purpose for us. It means listening to His voice and obeying His commands. It involves desiring and delighting in Him. It requires that, like Paul, we focus on the prize and run with all our strength. Ultimately, that's the best way to drown out the seductive strains of the world and sail safely toward home.

In *What I Believe*, the French novelist Francois Mauriac gives a candid account of his struggles with lust. The elderly Mauriac found that the golden years provided no reprieve from the battle. "Old age risks being a period of redoubled testing," he wrote, "because the imagination in an old man is substituted in a horrible way for what nature refuses him."[14]

In the book, Mauriac considers a number of arguments and defenses against lust that he'd learned during his religious upbringing, but found them all insufficient. In the end, he could find only one compelling reason for purity: "Blessed are the pure in heart, for they will see God." Why were Jesus' words so inspiring to him? Mauriac wrote, "Impurity separates us from God. The spiritual life obeys laws as verifiable as those of the physical world. . . . Purity is the condition for a higher love—for a possession superior to all possessions: that of God."[15]

Mauriac's story reminded me of what the nineteenth-century Scottish preacher Thomas Chalmers called "the expulsive power of a new affection." Chalmers believed that conquering sin wasn't just a matter of steely resolve or external controls; it was best accomplished by replacing sinful affections with holy ones. "A moralist will be unsuccessful in trying to displace his love of the world by reviewing the ills of the world," he preached. "Misplaced affections need to be replaced by the far greater power of the affection of the gospel."[16]

Mauriac found that guilt, discipline, even a fulfilling marriage couldn't hold up against the tidal wave of lust. He needed a new affection. Only the sweeter song of intimacy with God was enough for him to resist the siren song of lust.

WINNING THE PRIZE

When Paul died, it looked as though his life had been a failure.

The book of Acts closes with Paul under house arrest. We're told that during this stint, he was able to have visitors and "proclaimed the kingdom of God . . . without hindrance" (Acts 28:31). When he was eventually released, the tireless apostle hit the road again, visiting churches in Macedonia, Colossae, Crete, and Ephesus, where he was rearrested.

This second imprisonment was far worse than the first. He was chained "like a criminal" in his cell (2 Tim. 2:9). Some of his closest friends abandoned him and he knew he was going to die. "For I am already being poured out like a drink offering, and the time for my departure is near" (2 Tim. 4:6). He begged Timothy to come and visit him before winter. He wanted to see his son in the faith one last time. But most scholars believe the end came quicker than he anticipated and Paul was executed that summer. The final moments of Paul's life were unceremonious and brutal. The man who had spent decades traversing the dusty roads of the Roman Empire was likely led outside the city of Rome and beheaded in the street.

Yet that grim scene didn't tell the full story of Paul's life. In truth, his story was just beginning.

Paul's crazy dream to bring the message of Jesus beyond

the Jewish world had taken root. The Empire, which put Paul to the sword, would eventually embrace his message and spread it to the ends of the earth. Within a few hundred years, the majority of Romans would identify themselves as followers of the crucified Nazarene that Paul proclaimed.

Paul's life was anything but easy. He expended incredible energy and overcame towering obstacles. But it wasn't sheer force of will that enabled Paul to prevail. No, he tuned his ear to the sweeter song of the gospel and he ran with everything he had. From prison, he wrote these final words:

> I have fought the good fight, I have finished the race, I have kept the faith. Now there is in store for me the crown of righteousness, which the Lord, the righteous Judge, will award to me on that day. (2 Tim. 4:7–8)

Self-Control Training:
Entry #2—Making the Inventory

WHEN I ENLISTED MY WIFE TO HELP me in my attempt to improve my self-control, I wasn't sure exactly what to expect. After a couple of sighs and an eye-roll or two, she agreed to help me form this unusual inventory. And since she's just about the nicest person on the planet, she started with a cascade of compliments and qualifiers to offset the criticism.

"I appreciate that," I told her, "but I want you to be completely honest with me."

I was hoping she would name specific behavioral traits. *You start things, but don't finish them. You spend too much time on your phone. You leave your socks on the floor.* Maybe I was hoping she'd single out those kinds of behaviors because they're concrete and easy to target, if not to change. And maybe I was hoping she'd pinpoint those quirks because, while they're frustrating, they aren't exactly threatening. No one ever threw himself off a bridge because he wasn't tidy enough around the house. Unfortunately, she didn't mention any of those behaviors. No, she aimed her critique at the level of my soul.

"You're a really good man," she started, "and I know you love God. But . . ."

Her voice trailed off as she searched for the right words.

"Just tell me," I said.

"Well, sometimes I think you could stand to be a little more *spiritual*."

Ouch.

She pointed out (amid another avalanche of compliments and qualifiers) that while I spend a lot of time reading about God and talking about God, I don't seem to spend a ton of time *with* God.

"Really, I'm not trying to be critical," she said. "I'm weak in those areas too. I hope you aren't offended. See, I hate this."

It was hard to hear, but she was right. The truth is I tend to neglect many of the basic formative disciplines like Bible reading and prayer—those alone-with-God activities.

This helped me. Originally, I had my eye on more exotic disciplines. Maybe I'd start walking labyrinths or mastering *Lectio Divina*, an ancient style of Benedictine prayer. Alas, I've settled on a handful of prosaic but powerful practices: Bible reading, prayer, and (I'm bracing myself as I write this), fasting. Oh, and exercise. I'm going to start running. That may not sound superspiritual, but let's face it. If I'm going to improve my self-control, I need to get off the couch.

I thanked my wife for her help, but it turned out she had one more piece of advice.

"You need to start picking up your dirty socks, too."

Chapter 3

Meeting the Enemies

What Scripture Says about Fighting the Flesh and the Devil

"I do not understand what I do. . . . For I do not do the good I want to do, but the evil I do not want to do—this I keep on doing."

—ROMANS 7:15, 19

These words, written by the apostle Paul almost two thousand years ago, may be the most relatable in all of Scripture. Who hasn't muttered some form of them as they fall, for the thousandth time, to that old besetting sin? Or think them as they, yet again, leave a good deed undone, that expression of love unsaid? A lack of knowledge isn't always the culprit either. Like Paul, we often "know the good we ought to do." The problem is that we don't do it.

I know I don't. In the introduction to this book I confessed some of my deficiencies in this area. Well, "deficiencies" is a convenient euphemism, but it sounds more respectable than face-plant failures. The purpose of my confessing wasn't to hit you up for free counseling; I was trying to communicate something of the frustration (and surprise!) I feel when my behaviors fall short of my beliefs. I'm flabbergasted each time I give free rein to a destructive impulse or fail to do what's right.

I also mentioned my conviction that the biggest obstacle to improving in this area isn't usually a lack of resources or understanding. Rather, it's the tenacious enemy I encounter in the mirror every morning. In the famous words of the cartoonist Walt Kelly, "We have met the enemy, and he is us." Part of me wants to do the right thing. Yet another part really doesn't want to.

The frustrating thing is that my behavior often contradicts my most deeply held beliefs and values. It's like I have a split personality. When I flip to Romans 7, I could be reading my journal. "I have the desire to do what is right," Paul lamented, "but not the ability to carry it out" (ESV).

What's going on? Paul identified the reason for his predicament, and for ours. He strove to please God, but there was a saboteur in the ranks—sin. "But if I am doing the very thing I do not want, I am no longer the one doing it, but sin which dwells in me.... on the one hand I myself with my mind am serving the law of God, but on the other, with my flesh the law of sin" (Rom. 7:20, 25 NASB). As a result, Paul was a house divided, a walking civil war. "What a wretched man I am!" Paul wrote, exasperated at his failures. "Who will rescue me from this body that is subject to death?" (7:24).

THE DARK SIDE

So where did all this sin and dividedness come from? Answering that question requires taking a quick trip back to the first chapters of Genesis. Far before researchers were conducting self-control experiments in drab, windowless rooms, humanity's willpower was put to the ultimate test in a lush garden. It started out promising.

God created the first humans, Adam and Eve, in His image and appointed them stewards of His good creation. They enjoyed unbroken intimacy with their Creator and each other. They were given only one restriction: "you must not eat from the tree of the knowledge of good and evil, for when you eat from it you will certainly die" (Gen. 2:17). Call it the first self-control test of all time. And if you went to Sunday school, you know what happened.

They failed. Miserably. Eve bit the apple (or whatever the fruit was), Adam finished it off, and proceeded to blame his wife for the whole thing.

We've been biting and blaming ever since.

Whatever you think of the Genesis narrative, it's hard to deny its explanatory power. It makes sense of an age-old paradox we encounter in human nature. How can we be so selfless and splendid one moment and so sinful and stupid the next? Genesis provides a rather elegant answer. Our capacity for selflessness

We have an inborn tendency to mess up, to choose sin and selfishness over holiness and intimacy with God and each other.

and splendor comes from the fact that we were made in the image of God. Our sinfulness and stupidity? That traces back to the fall. Because of our ancient ancestors' fateful decision, there's a *bentness* to our nature. We have an inborn tendency to mess up, to choose sin and selfishness over holiness and intimacy with God and each other. It's what makes the business of controlling our behavior so difficult. Even when we desire to do what's right, we slam headlong into this internal barrier.

It's important not to underplay this reality. We might be tempted to say we're a tad mischievous, a bit naughty. But the reality Scripture describes is more sinister. The Bible states that our hearts are "deceitful" and "desperately wicked." Jesus described the heart as the birthplace of "evil thoughts—murder, adultery, sexual immorality, theft, false testimony, slander" (Matt. 15:19). It seems our hearts are crowded with destructive impulses straining for expression. And these destructive urges routinely win out. As theologian Marguerite Shuster writes, "the reservoir of evil in all of us is deeper than we know, and . . . barriers against its eruption are shockingly fragile."[1]

I'm sorry to go dark on you, especially this early in our journey together. But if we're going to understand why we fail to control ourselves, I believe we have to begin with an honest appraisal of human nature. And the truth is, though we like to dismiss evil as an antiquated notion or an external reality, the truth is more uncomfortable. It's alive and well. In you. And me.

I don't like it either. I'll gladly accept the made-in-God's-image part. That's elevating, dignifying. In fact, I can't imagine more auspicious origins. But this idea of being fallen is unpleasant. Are you telling me I have an inbuilt propensity for sin and selfishness and there's nothing I can do about it? That evil is somehow stitched into the fabric of my DNA? Actually, that's more than unpleasant. It's downright rude.

Of course I could always snap my Bible shut and turn on the TV or radio. There I'm likely to encounter a very different message about myself. I'll probably hear that I have unlimited potential, and that my troubles would disappear if I just believed in myself a little more. I certainly won't hear that I'm weak, flawed, or (gasp!) sinful. No, I'll be assured that I'm beautiful, powerful, and capable of achieving virtually anything. Just love myself and unleash my multisplendored awesomeness cuz baby I'm a firework!

Okay, I borrowed that last line from pop singer Katy Perry, but it illustrates my point. It captures the message we hear emanating from the broader culture, the one you hear articulated *ad nauseam* through songs and sitcoms and repeated by athletes, actors, and reality TV stars. And it can be very appealing, especially when set next to the Bible's rather grim assessment of human nature. I'd love to take refuge in this narrative and get down to the business of freeing the rainbowy goodness pent up in my heart. The only problem is I don't buy it. I've been at this being-a-human thing for four decades now and the evidence is in. I'm a son of Adam. I'm an apple-biter. I'm a blamer. Heck, just this morning I lost my shoes, and falsely accused my wife of hiding them! I know myself too well to deny the biblical truth about my nature. To quote another pop singer, Pink, who apparently has a more biblical worldview: "I'm a hazard to myself. Don't let me get me."

FAVORITE SINS, CROOKED TIMBERS

A few years ago, Barna research group conducted more than a thousand interviews with Americans of various ages and backgrounds.[2] The purpose of the study: to discover our biggest temptations and how we deal with them. Procrastinating (60 percent), worrying (60 percent), eating too much (55 percent), and spending too much time on media (44 percent) topped the list of most common temptations. More serious habits like viewing pornography (18 percent), lying or cheating (12 percent), abusing drugs and alcohol (11 percent), or doing something sexually inappropriate with someone (9 percent), were less common. Though, as the researchers pointed out, the results were likely skewed by people's reluctance to confess struggling with these more serious sins.

To me, the most disheartening finding of the study wasn't which temptations we fall for; it was that we have no idea why we do. The study found that half of the respondents didn't know why they succumbed to temptation. Others reported various reasons for their lapses, including a desire to feel less lonely or to satisfy people's expectations. Only 1 percent cited the role of human or sinful nature.

The study reveals a disconnect in our thinking. We know that we have a problem with temptation. According to the American Psychological Association, Americans consistently name a lack of willpower as their number one character deficit. Like Paul, we know we don't do the good we want to do. We realize we lack self-control, that we're weak. As the Barna study demonstrates, we easily identify the areas in which we fall to temptation. What we have no clue about is *why*. Barna President David Kinnaman offered this observation on the findings:

> Only 1% of Americans of any age are able to articulate that giving in to temptation might be caused by sin. Most Americans think of temptation more as a steady stream of highs and lows that must be navigated. This reveals a gap in biblical thought on the subject of temptation among the nation's population.[3]

Most of us know we're failing but have no idea what's behind our failures. When it comes to fighting sin, we're like a blind boxer— we keep getting hit, but don't know where the blows are coming from.

In the first chapter, we looked at different definitions of self-control. We saw the importance of delaying gratification and doing what's right, even when we don't feel like it. We also explored the biblical concepts related to self-control. They included the need to be sober and restrained, balanced and mastered. All of these definitions assume an inner conflict, a divided self. They imply the presence of an internal enemy. Unfortunately, most of us are oblivious to the battle, which virtually guarantees we will never win it.

In his book *The Road to Character*, David Brooks argues that we live in a post-character culture. We care more about success and achievements (what Brooks calls "résumé virtues") than we do about cultivating traits like honesty or faithfulness (what Brooks calls "eulogy virtues," the kind of qualities that get mentioned at your funeral).

Part of the reason for this shift, Brooks writes, is that we have strayed from a school of thought that saw people, not as inherently good, but as fundamentally flawed. Brooks dubs this the "crooked timber" tradition, a phrase he borrowed from the philosopher Immanuel Kant: "Out of the crooked timber of humanity, no straight thing was ever made."[4] According to this older view of human nature, we are not inherently good creatures who simply need more freedom and affirmation. Rather, we are splendid but damaged. Like crooked timbers, we need to be straightened.

Brooks writes that the crooked timber tradition was "based on the awareness of sin and the confrontation with sin."[5] And here's the surprising part. According to Brooks, it was this consciousness of sin that allowed people to cultivate virtue. That might seem like a strange argument. How could having a dim view of human nature enable people to become more virtuous? Because once they were conscious of their sinful nature, they could take steps to fight against it. "People in this 'crooked timber' school of humanity have an acute awareness of their own flaws and believe that character is built in the struggle against their own weaknesses," Brooks writes.[6] "Character is built in the course of your inner confrontation."[7] This inner confrontation is anything but easy, but the struggle is worth it. Brooks writes:

> Character is a set of dispositions, desires, and habits that are slowly engraved during the struggle against your own weakness. You become more disciplined, considerate, and loving through a thousand small acts of self-control, sharing, service, friendship, and refined enjoyment.[8]

Brooks believes that a failure to do this hard work has serious consequences. "If you don't develop a coherent character in this way, life will fall to pieces sooner or later. You will become a slave to your passions."[9]

Sinful, fallen, broken, crooked—whatever word you use, it's essential to face the warped side of our nature. If you believe you're essentially good, you'll be completely unprepared to combat the sinful impulses lurking in your heart. "Let anyone who thinks that he stands take heed lest he fall" (1 Cor. 10:12 ESV). Accepting the biblical vision of human nature arms you with a sober self-awareness. It makes you wary of your impulses and desires. It helps you realize that you need wisdom and divine help to resist temptation and pursue righteousness. Ultimately, it's the first step to leading a self-controlled life.

If you believe you're essentially good, you'll be completely unprepared to combat the sinful impulses lurking in your heart.

IS A FAILURE TO CONTROL YOURSELF ALWAYS A SIN?

Failures of self-control often result in sin. If you cheat on your spouse—or even on your taxes—you're guilty of sinning. But that's not true of all willpower failures. Eating a cookie instead of kale isn't evil; it just means your taste buds are working properly. Same with choosing to lounge around on a Saturday rather than lace up and run a marathon.

However, at some point, consistently taking the easy path does cross that blurry boundary into sin territory. Eating that cookie isn't a problem. But consume a whole box of cookies (which I'm ashamed to say I've done), and you're flirting with gluttony. Lounging around on a Saturday is fine. Do it every day, and you're guilty of sloth. You get the picture.

Throughout this book I talk about resisting behaviors that are clearly sinful and some that are simply shortsighted or counterproductive. Self-control is involved in avoiding both. And even when lapses in self-control don't result in explicit sin, that doesn't mean they're inconsequential. If unchecked, they can still have a destructive affect on your life. The apostle Paul wrote of some of these gray areas of his day. "'I have the right to do anything,' you say—but not everything is beneficial. 'I have the right to do anything'—but I will not be mastered by anything" (1 Cor. 6:12).

DESERT SHOWDOWN

So we have an enemy within, sabotaging our efforts to please God. As if that weren't bad enough, the Bible also warns of an external enemy of our souls. "Your enemy the devil prowls around like a roaring lion looking for someone to devour" (1 Peter 5:8). *Oh no*, you might think. *Is he really going to get all spooky and talk about Satan?* Well, yes, I do believe what the Bible says is true, that we have a spiritual adversary. I also believe that some Christians get downright weird about the topic, so I get your apprehension. They adopt a "devil made me do it!" mentality or start seeing a demon under every bush.

The Bible, however, is matter-of-fact in describing the devil— and in telling us what we must do to fight him. We're to arm ourselves with truth, righteousness, faith, salvation, the gospel, and God's Word (Eph. 6:10–18). Since Satan works in tandem with our fallen nature, we're instructed to avoid sinful or foolish behaviors that might give him a "foothold" in our life. In short, we defeat Satan by turning to God, and obeying His commandments.

Self-control plays a major role. Look at the broader context of the "roaring lion" passage above. "Be sober and *self-controlled*. Be watchful. Your adversary, the devil, walks around like a roaring lion, seeking whom he may devour" (1 Peter 5:8–9 WEB, emphasis mine). James commends a similar strategy. "Submit yourselves, then, to God. Resist the devil, and he will flee from you" (James 4:7). We don't need exotic tools or secret knowledge to defeat him. When we resist temptation, Satan flees.

Of course no one responded to a spiritual onslaught better than Jesus. The Bible tells us that Jesus was tempted in every way and yet did not sin (Heb. 4:15). The Gospels give us a front-row seat to an unusual showdown between Jesus and the enemy. Satan shows up when Jesus is alone in the wilderness and has been fasting for forty days. He knows Jesus is weak, depleted.

The first temptation: bread. "If you are the Son of God, tell these stones to become bread," Satan sneers. It's actually a two-pronged enticement. He's challenging Jesus to prove His divine identity and to satisfy His hunger. Jesus rebuffs Satan with words from Scripture. "Man shall not live on bread alone, but on every word that comes from the mouth of God" (Matt. 4:4).

Next, Satan leads Jesus to the pinnacle of the temple, and challenges Jesus to jump. He even quotes Scripture, promising that God will send angels to "lift you up in their hands, so that you will not strike your foot against a stone." It might sound like a silly stunt, but the sensational spectacle would validate Jesus' messianic identity in full view of the Jewish religious leaders. Again, Jesus parries with holy writ. "It is also written: 'Do not put the Lord your God to the test'" (Matt. 4:7).

Finally, Satan takes Jesus to a high mountain and shows Him all the kingdoms of the world. "All this I will give you," Satan says, "if you bow down and worship me" (Matt. 4:9). At this point, Jesus is fed up. "Away from me, Satan! For it is written: 'Worship the Lord your God, and serve him only'" (Matt. 4:10).

As I read this exchange, one thing stands out to me. *Satan's temptations are all shortcuts.* Think about it. What did Satan offer Jesus that He wasn't going to get in the long run anyway? Bread? The moment Satan leaves Jesus angels come to feed Him. Proof of His identity? Jesus knows He's the Son of God—He doesn't need to perform miracles to prove it. How about the kingdoms of the world? This too His Father would ultimately grant Him (Phil. 2:8–9). Everything Satan dangles in front of Jesus is something Jesus is going to get eventually anyway.

This doesn't mean Satan's temptations were easy to resist. Not at all. Their appeal lay in the promise that they could be obtained painlessly. Satan offers Jesus exaltation without the cross, vindication without faith. And it's immediate. He's promising them *now*. In resisting Satan, Jesus chooses the slower and more painful course that His Father has set for Him. Jesus knows it will require passing through hardship, rejection, and death. Ultimately, what Jesus will receive from His Father will vastly surpass anything Satan can offer. But it will require faith and humility, patience, and trust. Jesus opts for the slower, harder way.

I don't think Satan has changed his strategy. He offers the same shortcuts to us.

I don't think Satan has changed his strategy. He offers the same shortcuts to us. I've encountered them myself. For instance, I know if I obey God, I will be fulfilled. Jesus has come to give me an abundant life. God promises to "fill me with joy in [His] presence, with eternal pleasures at [His] right hand" (Ps. 16:11). But Satan sidles up to me, usually when I'm hungry, dissatisfied. "Why don't you just grab that fulfillment on your own right now?" he says. "It doesn't matter if it's a sin. You deserve it."

God has promised to clothe and feed me, to take care of my needs (Matt. 6:30–34). The One who owns "the cattle on a thousand hills" (Ps. 50:10) certainly has the resources to do it. Yet Satan plants doubts in my mind about this promised provision. "Will he really take care of you?" he whispers. "Maybe you better grasp for your own security, even if it means doing something dishonest."

The best way to head off such temptation is to follow Jesus' example. It starts with listening to His sermon—and not Satan's. It means countering the lies the enemy whispers in our ear with the unchangeable truth found in Scripture. And it requires trusting God and taking the longer, harder road to fulfillment. When we do those things, Satan runs for the exit.

Unfortunately, we don't always follow Jesus' example. We're weak, sinful. We're "crooked timbers." Sometimes we can't spot Satan's lies, let alone resist them. The good news is that we can make progress. As we'll see in the next chapter, with use, our spiritual muscles get stronger. As we follow the Victor in the wilderness, our self-control will continue to grow.

Self-Control Training:
Entry #3—Bible Reading

IF MY RESEARCH HAS TAUGHT ME anything, it's this: start small. Don't do too much right away and don't start too many things at once. The reason? It takes a lot of willpower to forge new habits, and your willpower is limited. I knew that if I woke up on Day One and tried to read a book of the Bible, pray for an hour, fast, and run three miles, I'd probably collapse from emotional and physical exhaustion—then take the next month off. Gradual beginnings might not be as exciting, but they are more effective. Because of this dynamic, I decided to tackle these disciplines one at a time.

First up: Bible reading. In the past I've been inconsistent in this area, and I want to start reading Scripture every single day. I decided to start with just fifteen minutes a day. I know, I know, don't hurt yourself, right? Fifteen minutes may not seem like much. But I've learned not to despise small beginnings. Once I have a habit of reading my Bible for fifteen minutes a day, I can build from there.

I downloaded an app on my phone that helps you read the Bible in one year. Every day the app features small samples from the Old and New Testaments. That way you don't have to spend a month plugging through Deuteronomy. Each day's readings take about fifteen minutes. I decided that I'd read the passages first thing in the morning. What better way to start the day than with God's Word? Should be easy, right?

Not exactly. The first morning, I reached for my phone fully intending to open my Bible app. Instead I found myself doing what I always do first thing in the morning—checking social media. After a few minutes on Twitter and Facebook, I opened my email. There were a couple work emails that needed my attention, and I started replying. Then a bleary-eyed three-year-old walked into our room and the morning began. It wasn't until later that day I realized I'd skipped my Bible reading altogether. The experience also taught me that before I could form a new, good habit, I had to break a bad one—checking social media and email first thing in the morning. Mindful of this tendency, on Day Two I managed to hold off on checking social media and read my Bible. But about half of the mornings, I'd revert to my old ways. Even when I was reading my Bible app on my phone, I'd feel the pull to check social media. Above I noted how Satan's temptations are all shortcuts. I'm not saying Twitter is demonic, but it's become something of a shortcut for me. It provides instant entertainment, connection, and affirmation—all without having to turn to God. Even if I managed to stay off Twitter, I'd open email or check the news. Even as I was reading through 1 Kings, I kept wondering what stories I'd missed while I'd slept. About half the time I'd opt for checking other things on my phone and deferring my Bible reading till later in the day. And later in the day rarely came.

My phone was a landmine of distractions, pulling me away from spending time in God's Word. After a couple weeks of spotty Bible reading, I realized what I had to do—go analog. I had thought my smartphone, with its accessibility and handy apps, was the key to regular Scripture engagement. In fact, it was the enemy. So I pulled my big black Bible off the shelf, lugged it up to my bedroom, and plunked it down on my nightstand. It literally shot up a little cloud of dust when it landed.

It was a good move, though. Now when I wake up, it's the first thing I see. I've had far more success reading this physical Bible than a digital one. In my research about habits, I learned about the importance of "cues," physical signals that trigger a behavior. Seeing that big black Bible every morning is a cue for me. And even though I still hear the siren song of social media, checking it requires closing the Bible and setting it down, something I'm less likely to do than simply swiping over to a different app on my phone.

Researchers identify some habits as "keystone habits," meaning that in addition to creating a healthy routine, they influence all areas of your life, encouraging other virtuous behaviors. I'm convinced Bible reading is a keystone habit (and we'll discuss that more in chapter 6). When I start my day in God's Word, the whole day is different. I have a better attitude, I'm more focused, and better equipped to resist temptation. I'm even nicer to my kids. Going forward, I know that starting the day in God's Word will be crucial to building self-control.

Chapter 4

Hope for Growth

How to Grow Your Puny Willpower Muscles

"The best way to think of willpower is not as some shapeless behavioral trait but as a sort of psychic muscle, one that can atrophy or grow stronger depending on how it's used."

—JEFFREY KLUGER

Did you have a sibling who drove you nuts growing up?

I did. For me it was my brother Dan. Even now I feel bad for being irritated with him. After all, Dan wasn't inconsiderate or mean. Though he was three years older than me, and much stronger, he never bullied me. But that was part of the problem. The reason Dan was so annoying was that Dan was perfect.

I remember getting angry with him for some reason—so angry that I curled my fingers into claws and swiped them across his bare chest. As four red lines appeared across his torso, I thought I'd finally done it. Surely this would be enough to make Dan throttle his little brother. Instead Dan pinched his eyes closed, took a sharp breath in, said, "I forgive you," and left the room.

See what I mean? Annoying.

When Dan was eight years old, he decided to give up sugar.

Just like that. It's odd enough for a kid to swear off sugar, and stranger still to actually do it. But Dan did. For five years! Not a slice of pie. Not a sip of Coke. Not even a jawbreaker candy from the gas station down the street. Nothing.

As we moved through our teens, my brothers and I all worked side jobs. For me and my other brothers, the money we made went out as quickly as it came in. Usually we squandered our paltry paychecks on anything we thought might impress girls: Polo shirts, Diesel jeans, Eternity cologne, and hairspray (hey, it was the '90s). But Dan saved his. Recently my mom commented on our different spending habits growing up. "You all spent your money as soon as you got it, or even before. Then you borrowed money from Dan."

Dan's perfection affected more than just eating and spending habits. He was a spiritual prodigy of sorts. He memorized reams of Scripture and sang like an angel in the church choir. Each night he bowed down and prayed beside his bed, which of course, he had made that morning.

Since we were pastor's kids, the story of Daniel in the Bible loomed large in my imagination. The Jewish Daniel was a paragon of character. He prayed with the regularity of a clock, three times a day, and refused to bow to idols. So stalwart was Daniel that not even threats of fiery furnaces or snarling predators could make him swerve from the path of righteousness.

In my mind, there was little difference between my older brother and his biblical namesake. My parents had named my brother well. It was like the ancient, Jewish Daniel had walked out of the lions' den and right into our living room.

Why do I bring up my brother Dan? Well, I didn't have the name for it back then. But essentially what Dan exhibited was excellent self-control, especially for someone so young. I'm betting he would have been one of the kids able to hold out in the marsh-mallow experiment. And sure enough, Dan's "life outcomes" have been favorable. He's a committed Christian and active in his church. He's a proverbial pillar of the community. He's a great family man. Recently, his oldest daughter visited and noncha-lantly mentioned that her dad had devotions with each of his four children every morning before heading to work.

Oh, and Dan's successful.

A few years ago, I ran into one of Dan's friends. He told me of how he'd attended a business conference where my brother was one of the featured speakers. The headliner of the conference was the Super Bowl–winning coach and bestselling author, Tony Dungy, but the friend informed me that the NFL great was over-shadowed. "Dungy was great," the man said. "But your brother's talk was the best of the conference by far."

Even as an adult, Dan is finding ways to irritate me.

All joking aside, I love my brother and I'm happy for him. But what if you're not like Dan? What if you were like one of those kids who crammed the marshmallow into his mouth the second the researcher left the room . . . and then asked for another one? What about the rest of us?

When I started researching for this book, there was a nagging fear in the back of my mind. What if self-control is something that's set at birth? It's not like my brother had decades to develop this essential trait. So what if self-control is like height, mid-digital hair (look it up), or eye color? What if it's dictated by your DNA and that's that? What if it's set in stone? What if the only way to become like Dan is to be born like him?

WEAK WILLPOWER

In chapter 1, we explored the concept of self-control. We looked at definitions from the Bible and psychology. I shared my working definition of self-control, that it's basically the ability to do the right thing, even when you don't feel like it.

In chapter 2, we examined how self-control isn't ultimately about us. We saw the importance of having a higher purpose and how "sanctified goals" actually fuel our efforts to live righteous lives.

In chapter 3, we looked at the shadowy side of human nature. We grappled with some unpleasant realities. Far from being the virtuous champions we imagine ourselves to be, we're fallible and fallen. Even when we want to do what's right, we find ourselves plagued by sinful desires.

Now we need to consider a different yet related topic: willpower. Willpower is the emotional energy needed to withstand temptation. From a strictly human perspective, it's what enables self-control. It's the fuel. Willpower is required for a range of activities, from resisting temptation to learning new tasks to making decisions to persevering in difficult circumstances. But willpower is limited. Often, we just don't have enough.

CONTROLLING YOUR INNER HOMER SIMPSON

The Bible uses the term "double-minded" (James 1:8). Now scientists are using it too. "Some neuroscientists go so far as to say that we have one brain but two minds," writes psychologist Kelly McGonigal.[1]

The first mind refers to a group of structures located deep in the center of your brain, known as the reward system. This region of the brain is activated when you are exposed to something desirable and urges you to pursue it. It's been called the Homer Simpson of the brain—all desire, no restraint.

Good thing there's the prefrontal cortex. Located right behind your forehead, this area of the brain is responsible for planning, decision-making, and regulating behavior. When people suffer injuries to this region, their behavior spirals out of control. Unable to control their desires, they become reckless and irresponsible. It's wise to engage in activities that keep your prefrontal cortex healthy, like exercise, prayer, meditation, performing mentally demanding tasks, and yes, exercising self-control. Desire isn't bad, but it must be kept in check. There's no getting rid of Homer. Just don't let him run your life.

I thought of willpower recently as I rewatched one of the all-time greatest comedy sketches. In the Mad TV clip, the comedian Bob Newhart plays a mild-mannered psychologist helping a young woman struggling to overcome her phobias.

Newhart's character sits opposite the patient in an office filled with wood paneling and tufted leather chairs. Then he invites her to share her problems. But when she does, Newhart's calm demeanor disappears. He leans forward, suddenly angry and shouts at the top of his lungs. "STOP IT!"

It's a hilarious skit (seriously, go watch it). We recognize the absurdity of the psychologist's approach, which provides a sharp contrast to the stereotype of the coddling therapist. I also think there's another reason the sketch is so effective. I wonder if part of us wants to believe that Hartman's "therapy" just might work. Maybe all we need to eliminate destructive behaviors is a blunt directive to do so. Perhaps we could overcome all of our issues, even gripping phobias, through sheer willpower alone. Maybe we can just "stop it!" Of course, another part of us realizes it isn't that simple. Yes, willpower is important, but it's limited. All too often, it isn't enough—but why?

A FINITE RESOURCE

About twenty years ago, researchers discovered something fascinating about willpower. It all started with a plate of warm chocolate chip cookies (no marshmallows this time) and a bowl of radishes. Those were the two choices set before college students in a landmark experiment conducted by psychologist Roy Baumeister. It was a setup from the beginning. The student volunteers had been fasting before they walked into a laboratory that was "filled with the delicious aroma of fresh chocolate and baking."[2] There on the table were the fresh cookies placed next to a bowl of red and white radishes.

Then they were given the rules. One group of students was permitted to eat only the radishes. The other was free to feast on the cookies. To heighten the temptation, researchers left the lab and watched the students from an adjacent room. The radish-only students eyed the cookies with longing. A few even picked up the forbidden treats and sniffed them before returning them to the plate.

Then the volunteers were led to another room where they were given a geometry puzzle to work on. They were told the puzzles were designed to test their intelligence. In reality the puzzle was impossible to solve. The experimenters wanted to see how long they would struggle with the puzzle before giving up. And that's where things got interesting. The participants who had eaten cookies dramatically outperformed those who had eaten radishes. It wasn't even close. Those who had consumed the delicious cookies struggled with the puzzle for about twenty minutes before calling it quits. The radish-eaters lasted only eight minutes, less than half as long.

Why the dramatic difference?

Resisting the cookies drained the participants' willpower. When it came time to solve a complicated puzzle, their reserves of willpower were dangerously low. Baumeister and his team had discovered that willpower is limited. It runs out. Baumeister dubbed the phenomenon "ego depletion."

What's more, Baumeister concluded that, "seemingly different, unrelated acts share a common resource."[3] That is, the same power it takes to resist cookies is what we use to push ourselves to solve math problems. Both tasks drew from the same source. "Making decisions uses the very same willpower that you use to say no to doughnuts, drugs or illicit sex," Baumeister writes. "It's the same willpower that you use to be polite or to wait your turn or to drag yourself out of bed or to hold off going to the bathroom."[4]

Baumeister's findings revolutionized the field. His original study has been cited in academic journals thousands of times and changed the way we think about self-control. Though some psychologists have challenged the concept of ego depletion, it is now widely accepted that willpower is a finite resource, one that can be depleted.

In some ways, such findings illustrate what the Bible teaches us about our nature—that we're finite beings with limited capacity. I think of Jesus' words to His disciples when He caught them napping on the eve of His crucifixion. "The spirit is willing, but the flesh is weak" (Matt. 26:41). Baumeister's findings provided empirical evidence that our willpower is weak—and that it gets weaker as we go.

Ego depletion has implications for battling temptation too. Actually, it means that "battling" temptation is usually a bad idea. It's easy to imagine that if we can fend off temptation once, we can do it again. But we're often weaker the second time 'round. Perhaps that's why Scripture urges us to "flee" temptation rather than stand and fight. Of course we can't always flee temptation. Sometimes we have to stand and fight. There's a reason the Bible instructs us to "put on the armor of God" and take up "the sword of the Spirit." But whenever possible, avoiding it altogether is wise. Petitioning God to "lead us not into temptation" is a better plan than trying to stare down sin.

FIXED OR FLUID?

To get my head around the concept of willpower, I interviewed sociologist and professor Bradley Wright. He opened our conversation with an odd statement.

"If I wanted to destroy your self-control, this is how I'd do it," he told me. "First, I'd make sure you got only three hours of sleep. Then I'd see to it that you got in a fight with your wife."

After making a mental note to never invite Dr. Wright to my house, I listened to his reasoning. The conflict and sleep deprivation would deplete my limited willpower reserves, pushing me into a vulnerable state. I'd be in the perfect position for my self-control to falter. This insight helped me make sense of past behavior. I realize now why I tend to eat poorly when I'm stressed. It's why I'm more likely to snap at my kids after a hard day at work. The radishes of stress and work leave little willpower for the puzzles of healthy eating and family life.

The big question I had for Dr. Wright, though, was the one inspired by growing up with a precocious brother. "Do some people naturally have more willpower than others?" I asked. His response was unequivocal.

> Absolutely! Some people just have a lot more self-control than others. My sister is an incredibly self-controlled person. She was doing aerobics in high school. She's a vegetarian. She was valedictorian. A champion tennis player. I could devote every second of the rest of my life to being self-controlled, and I wouldn't reach her.

Turns out the Good Professor had his own "Dan" growing up. It was nice that he could relate to my plight of being the slacker sibling, but I was hardly encouraged. What can those of us with naturally low self-control do about it? Wright went on to make an important distinction. He explained that there are two types of self-control that researchers study: *state* and *trait*.

State self-control, he explained, refers to a person's level of willpower moment to moment. And, like we've already seen, it varies. For example, maybe you woke up this morning determined to eat healthily. You had oatmeal and fruit for breakfast and planned to eat a salad at lunch. But then you had a busy morning at work and lunch got pushed back to 2:00 pm. By the time you finally got a moment to eat, you weren't too excited about the quinoa salad you'd packed and you found yourself drawn to the leftover pizza left in the break room. That morning your state self-control was high. You could have walked right by the pizza without much temptation. But after a stressful morning and a grumbling belly, things are different. Your state self-control is low, and you cave.

Trait self-control varies too, not from moment to moment but from person to person. Each person's self-control is affected by a host of factors but some people tend to have more of it than others. When I asked Wright about whether some people just naturally have more self-control, it's this second type of self-control I was referring to.

"Trait self-control is analogous to physical strength or the ability to run," he explained. "Some people are just going to be naturally stronger or faster."

Great, I thought. *The fix is in. Some people are naturally self-control triathletes and the rest of us are doomed to come in last.*

But Wright made a good point by extending the metaphor. "Just because someone is naturally stronger or faster than you, doesn't mean you don't go to the gym. Self-control is like a muscle. The more you work it, the stronger it gets." Good point. There are those rare people who stay thin and muscular despite never working out, but they're the exceptions. In order to be strong and healthy most of us have to eat well and exercise, especially as we get older. Cursing these athletic outliers from the couch might be cathartic but doesn't make much sense. Apparently, it's the same with self-control. We can complain about the Dans of this world . . . or we can start building our self-control muscles.

As Wright continued talking, I started to realize muscle was probably the best metaphor for understanding self-control. Elsewhere Wright wrote, "Self control is like a muscle. It weakens immediately after use, but it strengthens with frequent use."[5]

That's good news. Regardless of how much self-control you have naturally, it turns out there's an awful lot you can do to improve it.

COOL YOUR FUTURE "HOT" HEAD

One reason our willpower fails? We don't think it will. When it comes to forecasting how we'll behave in a moment of temptation or difficulty, we wildly overestimate our resolve. "When we imagine our future selves, it's almost like we're imagining a super hero," writes Colin Robertson, a researcher in performance psychology. "We envision someone who laughs in the face of temptation, someone who has boundless energy and unlimited time to boot."[6] There's a neurological basis for this phenomenon. One brain-imaging study showed that when people think about their future selves, the areas of the brain typically associated with thinking about oneself were unengaged. Instead, when they contemplated their future selves, their brains behaved identically to when they thought about other people.[7] We tend to think very highly of these foreign future selves. As the psychologist Kelly McGonigal writes, "Future you always has more time, more energy, and more willpower than present you."[8]

Of course, when temptation or difficulty comes, our future selves vanish and we find we're all too human. So why the rosy and unrealistic forecast? It's partly due to a phenomenon called the "hot-cold empathy gap." When we're calm and comfortable, in a "cool" state, we assume resisting future temptations will be a breeze. But then life happens. The kids start screaming. You skip a meal. You get a bad sleep. Work gets crazy. Suddenly you're in a "hot state," and much more likely to given in to temptation you would have easily resisted in a cooler state. They call it the heat of the moment for a reason! Hot states change our minds—literally. When you're in a hot state, the reward centers of the brain become more active, making us easy marks for temptation.[9]

So what can you do to avoid falling prey to your hot head? The best strategy is to avoid heated situations altogether. Get enough sleep. Take a break. Walk away. Breathe. But let's face it—sometimes avoiding hot states just isn't possible. When your coworker or kids are driving you nuts, taking off isn't usually an option. In those cases, steal a move from Starbucks. The coffee chain giant came up with a way to help employees deal with cranky, precaffeinated customers. Starbucks's training manual leads baristas through an "If-Then" exercise. They're told to complete the following sentence: "When a customer is unhappy, my plan is to . . ." By planning their response to this inevitable scenario (while in a cool state), they're much more likely to respond well when it actually occurs. It's a form of preloaded decision-making that can be adapted for other hot-state situations.

Identify situations in which you've fallen prey to temptation, and then write out a plan for how you'll react to those situations in the future. That way when the moment arrives, you can default to your plan rather than falling prey to your impulses. So try to avoid hot states in the first place. If that's not possible, formulate a plan. Oh, and never grocery shop when you're hungry.

GROW, CONSERVE, REPLENISH

How can we strengthen our willpower? Just like we strengthen our muscles—with resistance. In other words, if you want to grow your willpower, start doing hard things. Read a challenging book. Go for a run. Learn a foreign language. Have an awkward conversation with a stranger. It all takes willpower and the more you do it, the easier it will become. Not only will you get better at the specific task; the growth in willpower you gain will enable you to push harder in all activities requiring effort. Even frivolous activities that take intentional effort can help. One study showed that people who used their nondominant hand saw increased self-control when it came to tackling other tasks as well.[10] When exercised, willpower grows.

Of course you still have to use your willpower wisely. You can grow your willpower, but it still wears out. Even bodybuilders' muscles fatigue. Triathletes get tired eventually. It's the same with your willpower. It's a precious commodity that you want to spend carefully. Wright warned me that conflict and lack of sleep compromise willpower. He also identified other "willpower wasters" like frequent use of social media and multitasking. In the future I need to be aware of these activities and limit them or avoid them altogether.

Recognizing that I have limited reserves of willpower enables me to be more strategic about how I expend it. When it comes to important tasks, I need to preserve enough willpower to accomplish them. There's one task that takes a lot of willpower for me: writing. It's hard! Some people say they love writing. But if I'm honest, I love *having* written. It takes a lot of discipline just to sit down in front of my computer and wrestle words into sentences for extended periods of time. On top of the actual challenge of writing, it's difficult to find the time to do it. I have a demanding day job and three noisy children. If you're picturing me writing this book in a quiet cabin by a lake, I'm sorry to disappoint you. Most often I write on evenings and weekends while kids pop in and out of my office asking for juice or screaming complaints, like "my brother bit me!"

For a long time, I put off writing till after work. I'd finish up the last task of the day, pour a fresh cup of coffee, and open my Word file. Here I go! But nothing happened. After a full day of answering emails, editing manuscripts, and sitting through meetings, I was spent. The blinking cursor on the blank page would mock me. My willpower was gone. After reading about willpower, I changed my routine. I started writing in the morning, before work, when my willpower reserves were high. It was a sacrifice (I'm writing these words at 7:30 a.m. on a Saturday morning), but it was worth it. I found I made much more progress.

I've also become more conscious about saving willpower for family life. On more than one occasion, my wife has told me that she feels like she and the kids "get the leftovers," that I'm tired and irritable in the evenings after work. Now I'm trying to preserve willpower for the evening hours by scheduling difficult meetings or challenging tasks for earlier in the day. If I fill my afternoons with less challenging assignments, I'm not spent when I sit down for dinner with my family.

So we can grow our willpower, and we need to conserve it. We also need to replenish it. Some of these strategies are common sense. Getting a good night's sleep goes a long way toward restoring your willpower reserves. Studies show that people who are well rested demonstrate far greater self-control than people who skimp on sleep. Eating well is also key. Tasks that expend willpower (even if they're not physically demanding) cause your blood glucose levels to drop. Researchers routinely use sugar pills or sweet drinks to combat the effects of ego depletion. But sugar is only a short-term fix and can actually sabotage your willpower long-term. Yes, sugary snacks provide an initial spike of blood sugar but they also cause us to release insulin, which then lowers blood sugar. That's why Bradley Wright identifies refined sugars and processed grains as the worst foods for willpower. Instead he advises eating "low-glycemic foods, those that keep steady blood sugar levels."[11]

Studies have shown meditation is a powerful way to build and replenish willpower. And you don't need to be a pro to reap the benefits. In fact, novices see greater results because it takes greater exertion. The effort required to still your mind strengthens willpower and even changes the way your brain operates. "Neuroscientists have discovered that when you ask the brain to meditate, it gets better not just at meditating, but at a wide range of self-control skills, including attention, focus, stress management, impulse control, and self-awareness."[12]

Some Christians are understandably wary of meditation. Many popular forms of meditation incorporate beliefs and practices from Eastern religions. Yet there is also biblical meditation. For centuries Christians have used contemplative prayer (which involves the silent repetition of a sacred word or sentence). Others choose simply to meditate on Scripture, mulling over a short section of the Bible. In addition to the rich spiritual rewards these practices bring, the benefits for willpower are dramatic.

Pastor and brain science expert, Charles Stone describes another way biblically minded Christians practice meditation:

Mindfulness is a spiritual discipline akin to biblical meditation that I practice as part of my daily devotional time. It's setting aside a time to be still before God to be in His presence in the present moment. It's not emptying our mind, but filling our mind with thoughts of Him and His Word. It helps us disengage from automatic thoughts, feelings, memories, and reactions and simply be in God's presence.[13]

Stone pointed out that just in the last year there were over four hundred studies published showing the brain benefits of mindfulness, including increased volume in the areas of the brain responsible for self-regulation.

Prayer is another proven way to replenish willpower. It prevents willpower from being depleted in the first place. A 2014 study divided subjects into two groups. One group prayed and one group did not. Then participants from both groups underwent activities designed to deplete their willpower and were given a test after. The non-prayers performed poorly on the test. Their willpower had been compromised by the exercises. But the praying subjects showed no loss of willpower. It was a shocking discovery. The researchers concluded that "Personal Prayer Buffers Self-Control Depletion."[14] While prayer is not a magic bullet that can be exploited for increased willpower, this research supports the scriptural truth of the power of prayer and its necessity for sustaining willpower.

Of course, as Christians, we're not surprised by such findings. We know that prayer is powerful. Scripture instructs us to "pray without ceasing" (1 Thess. 5:17 NASB). Jesus connected prayer to self-control when He commanded His disciples, "Watch and pray so that you will not fall into temptation" (Matt. 26:41). In light of what both Scripture and science teach us about the topic, praying may benefit us as much as the people for whom we pray.

GROWING YOUR SPIRITUAL MUSCLES

Peter is one of my favorite characters in the Bible. Part of why I'm drawn to him, honestly, is because of how imperfect he was, how relatable. He had high aspirations but couldn't seem to follow through. In other words, he had terrible self-control.

When the disciples spot Jesus walking on the water, it's Peter who springs out of the boat. He wants to walk on water, just like Jesus. Talk about high aspirations! Things go well for the first couple of shaky steps, but then his faith falters and he drops below the waves.

On another occasion, when Moses and Elijah supernaturally appear beside Jesus, Peter can't keep his mouth shut and blurts out the bizarre suggestion that they throw up a few tents and make it a campout. On the eve of Jesus' crucifixion it's Peter who brags that he'll never abandon Jesus, even if everyone else does. Then, that very night, Peter runs away when Jesus is arrested and he denies knowing Him. Three times!

Peter had his shining moments. His walking on water debut didn't end well, but he had the faith to at least try. He was also the first to articulate the true identity of Jesus, even if he was also quick to deny that he even knew who Jesus was. Peter had the right convictions and he felt them deeply. What he lacked was the ability to carry through on them, a classic case of low self-control. Jesus named His hapless disciple "Cephas," which means, "rock." I imagine Jesus smiling as He gave Peter this ironic nickname. In truth Peter was anything but solid and dependable.

But Peter changed. And most of that change happened in the aftermath of the events described in the gospel narratives. When we see Peter a couple of decades later, we can barely recognize him. He's referred to as an esteemed pillar, the leader of the church in Rome. He writes warm, fatherly letters to the fledging believers under his care, encouraging them to grow in godliness and to endure suffering. Peter had finally become the rock Jesus saw in a fumbling fisherman. The church historian Eusebius tells us that Peter met his death at the hands of the Roman emperor Nero. Peter was crucified, but they accommodated his one last request: that he be crucified upside down because he said he wasn't worthy to die in the same way as his Lord.

Self-control is a vital link. It's what enables us to persevere and attain godliness. Ultimately it culminates in love.

In his second letter to the church, Peter exhorted the early Christians to grow in maturity. Reminding them that they "participate in the divine nature," he urged them to "make every effort to add to your faith goodness; and to goodness, knowledge; and to knowledge, self-control; and to self-control, perseverance; and to perseverance, godliness; and to godliness, mutual affection; and to mutual affection, love" (2 Peter 1:4–7).

I find it interesting that Peter included self-control in the middle of this chain of spiritual growth. Perhaps he remembered what a challenge it was for him to develop this crucial virtue. By this stage in his life, he realizes it's a vital link. It's what enables us to persevere and attain godliness. Ultimately it culminates in love.

When I think about how Peter changed, I'm inspired. If that

early, erratic follower of Jesus could become a paragon of self-control, then maybe there's hope for me too. Peter wasn't a super saint. He was an ordinary person with a spotty track record of faithfulness. But as he walked with Jesus, he eventually became the person Jesus knew he could be. He grew. As we walk with Jesus, we will grow too.

Self-Control Training:
Entry #4—Prayer

THE NEXT DISCIPLINE I DECIDED to tackle was prayer. Talking to God right after reading my Bible just made sense. After listening to God's Word, it seemed natural to respond. It's not like I didn't pray already. But like my Bible reading, my prayer life is meager and inconsistent. I wanted to start praying every day.

As a pastor's kid, I grew up on stories of legendary prayer warriors. I recall hearing of revivalists whose knees literally wore ruts in wood floors as they petitioned the Almighty. I remember the famous quote from the reformer Martin Luther, who declared, "I have so much to do that I shall spend the first three hours in prayer."[15] When I was twenty, I read the biography of Reese Howells, a man who as a missionary in South Africa saw thousands of converts before returning to his native Wales to found a Bible college. Yet these activities were sidelines for Howells. His real vocation was prayer. According to his wife, he often spent twelve hours a day interceding for others.

Such stories are inspiring, but I'm going to be honest: when it comes to my own prayer life, they're demotivating. They bring a fresh wave of shame about my own prayerlessness. Rather than inspiring me to pray more, they make me think, *why bother?* So, I've decided to set such stories aside and take the same tack I did with Bible reading—start small, just fifteen minutes a day.

I chose to follow a formula. It was easy to remember thanks to a handy acronym: ACTS (Adoration, Confession, Thanksgiving, Supplication). And though it didn't seem very spiritual, I set a timer. I got right down on my knees in my office. (Fortunately, since I work from home, I can afford to look like a weirdo.)

On the first morning, I moved through the four phases of prayer quickly, praising God's for His attributes, confessing my sins, thanking God for the blessings in my life, and finally, making requests for God's help. The timer still hadn't gone off, so I kept going. My mind started to wander, and the thought hit me: the timer on my phone isn't working. It felt like I'd been praying forever! Getting up from the floor, I went over to my phone and took a peek. It was working all right . . . but it had only been eleven minutes. Clearly, when it comes to prayer, I have some growing to do. But I'm not discouraged. I know that while my willpower may be limited, it can grow. And mostly, I've been encouraged by the characters in Scripture. Most of them started off stumbling but ended up crossing the finish line anyway.

Chapter 5

The Transforming Power of Habits

Making Self-Control Automatic

"The orientation of the heart happens from the bottom up, through the formation of our habits of desire. Learning to love (God) takes practice."

—JAMES K. A. SMITH

What did you do today?

Did you have a shower? Brush your teeth? Get dressed? (I hope so.) Did you make coffee? Pack lunches? Exercise? Drop off the kids? Drive to work? Come home? Turn on the TV?

What if I told you that you didn't do any of those things? Because the truth is, you didn't. At least not in the sense of doing them as intentional actions, with forethought and purpose. You probably did them out of habit.

If you could review video footage of your average day, for the most part you wouldn't witness a person attentively navigating the world, pausing to make decisions each time they acted. You'd see someone moving about rather seamlessly, performing tasks without hesitation. You would see someone operating largely out of habit.

What exactly is a habit? According to Charles Duhigg, author of *The Power of Habit*, "a habit is a behavior that starts as a choice, and then become a nearly unconscious pattern."[1] These unconscious patterns determine a lot of our behavior. A Duke University study found that more than 40 percent of our actions come from habit rather than decisions. That means nearly half of our actions on any given day take place without much conscious thought. We just do them. They're habits.

Take the task of merging onto a freeway. The first time I did it, I was terrified. The fact that I was learning to drive in my dad's 1987 Cadillac didn't help. The thing was so big it felt more like steering a ship than driving a car. My knuckles whitened as my fists clenched the wheel. I checked the position of my hands. Ten and two, just like Dad said. As I rolled down the on-ramp, my torso straightened. My eyes darted between the car in front of me and the freeway. Each action took conscious thought. Shoulder check. Turn the blinker on. Gently press the gas pedal. Turn the wheel. When I finally settled into the flow of traffic, I breathed a sigh of relief. But I didn't get too comfortable. I had to constantly check to see if I was staying in my lane.

Today, after driving for more than twenty years, the experience of merging onto a freeway is quite different. Actually, it's not much of an experience at all. Yes, I perform the motions required to thread a three-thousand-pound vehicle into moving traffic, but I'm only vaguely aware of the fact that I'm hitting the gas, shoulder-checking, and signaling. In fact, while I'm doing these things, my mind might be somewhere else. I could be stewing about a bad day at work or singing along to the radio or threatening a noisy child in the backseat. The actions of merging onto the freeway have become a habit.

Don't be too impressed by my merging mastery. There's a simple neurological reason for why what once took effort now requires virtually none. In a process neuroscientists call "chunking" my brain has taken the sequence of behaviors involved in driving a car and turned them into an automatic routine.

The conscious, effortful thought it took to learn how to merge took place in the frontal lobes of my brain known as the prefrontal cortex. That's the executive region of our brains, the gray matter involved in making decisions and carrying out purposeful actions. When scientists do brain scans on people who are learning a new task, this region lights up like a Christmas tree. The prefrontal cortex is working overtime to learn how to do something unfamiliar. But as someone gets better at a task, that region goes dark. Why? Because once a behavior becomes habit, it's relegated to a small region deep in the center of our brains called the basal ganglia. Once the habit is safely stored in this region of the brain, it frees the prefrontal cortex to tackle other novel tasks. This explains why you're able perform repetitive behaviors (like driving) even while your mind roams to other topics. Your brain constantly seeks to turn behaviors into habits to save effort. This process frees up your prefrontal cortex to concentrate on unfamiliar and difficult tasks.

So what do habits have to do with self-control?

A lot. Remember the research about willpower we discussed in the last chapter? We learned that it's a finite resource. Expend enough willpower by tackling difficult tasks or resisting temptation and eventually your willpower reserves will run dry. You can build your willpower. You can be strategic about how you use it. But ultimately you only have so much. That's where habits help. Once a behavior becomes encoded as a habit, it no longer requires effort. Habits allow you to move behaviors from being conscious and effortful to unconscious and effortless. You outsource the work of willpower to the factory of habit.

Habits aren't confined to mechanical tasks like driving. They influence our moral and spiritual behavior as well. It's by creating healthy habits that we ultimately rise above the tide of continuous temptations and live virtuously. As theologian N. T. Wright stated, "Virtue is what happens when wise and courageous choices become second nature."

Willpower is still crucial, but habits are more reliable. If two people face the same temptation and one has made a habit of resisting that temptation and the other is depending on sheer effort to fend it off, guess which person is going to cave most of the time? The willpower guy or gal will give in far more often than the one relying on good habits. Whether it is resisting temptation or following through on a promise or completing a difficult task, bet on habits every time. Habits are so powerful they can even override our conscious choices. One study demonstrated that even when people write out a list before grocery shopping they often end up buying different foods once they get to the store. Why? The written plan wasn't enough to override their habits and change what they had bought in the past. Even shoppers who were trying to lose weight dumped their favorite desserts into their carts.[2]

The key to living a holy life isn't simply to out-battle temptation at every turn. It's to build righteous patterns into your life.

"I value self-discipline," said business guru Tim Ferriss. "But creating systems that make it next to impossible to misbehave is more reliable than self-control."[3] Pastor John Ortberg is more blunt: "Habits eat willpower for breakfast."[4]

If habits are truly that powerful,

the key to living a holy life isn't simply to out-battle temptation at every turn. It's to build righteous patterns into your life. It's achieved through habits.

INFORMATION ISN'T ENOUGH

Unfortunately, we're not accustomed to thinking about spiritual growth in terms of habits. We tend to believe that if we simply learn the right things, our behavior will change. Sin is the result of ignorance, we reason. We do stupid things because we don't realize that what we're doing is wrong.

At first blush, this kind of reasoning makes sense. And certainly, we need a certain modicum of knowledge to be able to choose to do what's right. But there's a problem: knowledge doesn't always lead to change. Even when we know what's right, we often still fail to do it.

I remember seeing a nurse out on his break smoking! When I saw him lighting up, perhaps having just left the room of someone dying of lung cancer, I wondered what was going through his mind as he inhaled the carcinogenic fumes. How can someone engage in that kind of risky behavior when they know full well the dire consequences of doing so? They know better than the rest of us the health risks posed by smoking, yet somehow that understanding hasn't helped them make the necessary changes to ditch that habit. It's hard to fathom, but it happens all the time. Knowledge doesn't always translate into action.

CIGARETTES AND VEGGIES

In the 1990s, a group of students in Washington participated in an eight-year anti-smoking program. Over that time, students were thoroughly educated on the many harmful effects of smoking, including the increased risks of diseases like COPD, cancer, and heart disease. Educators caught up with the students who participated in the study and compared the rate of regular smokers with a control group that did not participate in the program. Of the group that went through the program, 25.4 percent smoked regularly. In the control group, 25.7 percent now smoked. That means receiving nearly a decade of education on the life-threatening effects of smoking caused a paltry 0.3 percent reduction in the percentage of kids who went on to embrace the habit.[5] I don't know how many millions of dollars were spent on the long-term initiative, but if taxpayers knew about the abysmal results, I'm sure they'd want their money back.

It's not just anti-smoking campaigns that suffer from overestimating the impact of information. Do you remember the "5 A Day" campaign? It was a crusade run by across North America to try and get people eating the daily 400 grams of fruit and vegetables the World Health Organization recommended. Perhaps you recall seeing the colorful posters displaying a bounty of fresh produce. They were ubiquitous: in school classrooms, in workplace break rooms, on the sides of buses, in magazines, on TV. On one hand, they were extremely effective. To this day if you ask people how many fruits and veggies they're supposed to eat every day, most can provide the correct answer. But before you break out the broccoli to celebrate, consider this: though the campaign succeeded in teaching us information about nutrition, it didn't cause people to eat more fruits and vegetables. In fact, after the campaign, consumption of fruit and vegetables declined. In his book *The Social Animal*, David Brooks summarizes survey findings from the decades of social science research and concluded: "information programs alone are not very effective in changing behavior."[6]

This same principle holds true in our spiritual lives. Often our theological knowledge doesn't affect the way we actually live. We may go to church year after year, read the Bible, and study theology—and fail to change. Witnessing that disturbing disconnect in my own life is what drove me to write this book. I believe that knowledge is crucial; it just isn't enough.

Philosopher James K. A. Smith has reflected at length on this topic. Why do we believe that knowledge is enough to change us? He traces that idea back to the seventeenth-century philosopher René Descartes, who defined the human person as *res cogitans*, a "thinking thing." According to Smith, because of Descartes's broad influence on Western culture, most Christians continue to share this view of human nature, which discounts feelings and ignores physicality.

Like Descartes, we view our bodies as (at best!) extraneous, temporary vehicles for trucking around our souls or "minds," which are where all the real action takes place. In other words, we imagine human beings as giant bobblehead dolls: with humungous heads and itty-bitty, unimportant bodies.[7]

For Smith this elevation of the human intellect has implications for the Christian life. "'I think, therefore I am,' Descartes said, and most of our approaches to discipleship end up parroting his idea," he writes.[8]

As I read Smith's ideas, red flags were flying up all over the place. I'm a theology geek and a word nerd. You could say knowledge is kind of my thing. And I believe knowledge of God is important, so important I'm still paying off the loans I took out to attend seminary. One of my favorite quotes is from A. W. Tozer: "What comes into our minds when we think about God is the most important thing about us."[9]

As if anticipating my objections, Smith writes, "Well, how's that working out for you? . . . Has all of your new knowledge and information and thinking liberated you from those habits?"[10]

Point taken. Plus, as Smith goes on to explain, he doesn't dismiss the need for sound doctrine or clear thinking. He just argues knowledge alone isn't enough to form Christians who consistently act out what they believe. Pastor Todd Hunter agrees, writing, "Information alone does not produce change because it does not touch the will, the emotions, the heart, the spirit, or our social environment."[11] Even Paul acknowledges the point implicitly. After all, in Romans 7 he writes that he *knew* the good he ought to do. Yet despite having this knowledge of what was good, he found himself unable to do it.

Some people believe that if only they get a better grasp of God or the nature of the gospel, they will automatically transform. They're right to place a high premium on Christian truth. Understanding who God is and who we are enables us to embark on the journey toward change. It lights the path as we go.

But experiencing transformation takes more than mere

information. You could study the violin for years, read up on the instrument's history, and develop a sophisticated understanding of its mechanics. Yet if you never picked one up, you'd still be a lousy violinist. All of your knowledge wouldn't mean squat. In a similar way even the most ac-

Even the most accurate, in-depth understanding of scriptural truth won't produce change in and of itself. It must be internalized and put into action.

curate, in-depth understanding of scriptural truth won't produce change in and of itself. It must be internalized and put into action.

So if knowledge alone isn't the key to transformation, what is? According to Smith, "We don't need *less* than knowledge; we need more. We need to recognize the power of habit."[12]

GOOD HABITS, BAD HABITS

As we've seen, habits influence all kinds of behavior. It's not just mundane activities—like driving, dressing, and brushing your teeth—that are influenced by habit. It's more complex and important behaviors too. A whole range of activities gets programmed into our lives. Once they're in place, they take very little effort to continue. And that can be a bad thing.

I travel to Chicago every couple of months for work. Whenever I land in the Windy City, I find myself driven, as if by unseen forces, into a deep-dish pizza restaurant. My recent visit was no exception. As soon as I stepped off the plane, I began craving copious amounts of cheese covered in chunky tomato sauce. And sure enough, soon I found myself in Lou Malnati's pizzeria awaiting my handmade pizza pie with giddy anticipation.

It was sort of a sad scene. I was dining by myself, so there was no pretext of community; I was just there to gorge myself on pizza. And that's precisely what I did. After a few slices I hit a wall but consumed one more. There I was, filled with cheese and regret. As I maneuvered my distended belly away from the table, I swore that I wouldn't be back. But I will. That's the power of habit.

I believe a lot of our repetitive failures are the result of habit. I go to sleep fully intending to start the next day with prayer and devotions. Instead I wake up and instinctively reach for my phone and check social media. I plan to do one thing—but then do something different altogether. What in the world in going on? It's completely perplexing, until you understand the power of habit. The Bible has a vivid description for this kind of behavior. "As a dog returns to its vomit, so fools repeat their folly" (Prov. 26:11). It's a nauseating image, but it captures something of the stubborn nature of bad habits. For the fool, folly is so ingrained he can't help himself. He keeps returning to his behavior, no matter how dumb or disgusting it may be.

When we use the word "habit" we usually envision negative behaviors: smoking, swearing, chewing your nails, or eating too much deep-dish pizza. But of course there are good habits too. Often we don't think of them as habits. Perhaps it's a way to offload guilt. The bad things we do are unconscious, uncontrollable. The good things we do, we want to take credit for, so we chalk them up to good choices. Yet all kinds of our behaviors are the result of habit.

Since I confessed my pizza addiction, let me balance things out with a little bragging. I go to church. Every Sunday. I know that doesn't make me Christian of the Year. But, hey, in a time of dwindling church attendance, at least I'm showing up! It's not easy to get to church either. In order to make it to the service on time, my wife and I have to wake up early, get some coffee into our bloodstreams, and then face the real challenge: coaxing our three young children through the painstaking ballet of getting dressed, fed (oh no, Mary spilled yogurt on her dress . . . let's change her), hair combed, and out the door in a timely manner.

Even once we perform the minor miracle of getting the whole family into the van in time, we have a twenty-minute drive to get to our church. Since we attend a congregation in the urban core of the city, parking is always a nightmare. Most Sundays I duck into the sanctuary, wet from the Portland rain, dragging a stubborn child behind me. Yet somehow we get to church every week.

You might think I have to psych myself up to go through this routine. Summon every ounce of willpower in order to make the decision to go. But I don't. Truth be told, I don't even think about it. I just go.

Why? It's an ingrained pattern. I've been going to church all my life. Sleeping in on Sunday mornings would feel weird. Now don't get me wrong. Gathering with fellow believers each week to worship God is important to me. And my wife and I want to raise our kids in the church. We place a high value on worshiping with our brothers and sisters in Christ. But honestly, when I'm trudging through the motions Sunday morning in a barely conscious fog, I'm not thinking of much. And I'm doing it more or less on autopilot. We just go. It's a habit.

If attending church weren't a habit for me, I'd have to expend a lot of willpower each week just to get there. If I'm used to sleeping in each Sunday, I may even forget about church and have to set a reminder. Maybe I'd have to adjust my work schedule to carve out time off on Sunday. I'd have to steel myself to get the kids ready and explain to children used to playing on Sunday morning that they had to squeeze into dressier-than-normal clothes and comb their hair. Then I'd have to punch the church's address into my phone and try to figure out the tricky parking situation. If I'd had a particularly difficult week, I likely wouldn't have the willpower reserves to push through all those barriers. But since attending is a habit for me, I don't have to.

That's just one habit, albeit an important one. The power of habit can be leveraged to build all kinds of healthy practices into our life, like regular prayer, Bible reading, and acts of service. Habits can be vehicles for transformation. They help us build practices into our lives that cultivate virtue and free us from sin.

BILLY GRAHAM'S SPIRITUAL HABITS

After the famous evangelist Billy Graham died, author Jerry Jenkins recalled a private conversation he had with the late evangelist.[13] Jenkins, who assisted Graham in writing his memoirs, had interviewed Graham to collect material. Jenkins remembered how Graham waved away his first question.

"People look to you as a spiritual leader, a model, almost like the Protestant Pope—"

Graham interrupted him.

"They really mustn't do that. When I think of the number of times I've failed the Lord, I feel this low," Graham said, reaching out his hand and placing it flat on the floor.

Jenkins made several more attempts to ask a question based on Graham's revered status, but Graham "would have none of it."

Then Jenkins asked, "Well, just tell me how you maintain your own spiritual disciplines."

"Finally, I had hit on something he was eager to talk about," Jenkins recalled.

"He leaned forward, boring in on me with those piercing blue eyes. 'The Bible tells us to pray without ceasing and to search the Scriptures. And I do that.'"

"You pray without ceasing?" Jenkins asked.

"I do," Graham said, "and I have every waking moment since I received Christ at age 16. I'm praying right now as I'm talking to you that everything I say will glorify Christ."

Next Jenkins asked Graham about his habit of searching the Scriptures.

"Wherever I am in the world, in someone's home, my home, a hotel room, here in my office, anywhere, I leave my Bible open where I'll notice it during the day. Every time I see it, I stop and read a verse or two, or a chapter or two, or for an hour or two. And this is not for sermon preparation; it's just for my own spiritual nourishment."

Jenkins asked how he gets back into the habit when he misses a day or two. The evangelist "cocked his head and squinted."

"I don't think I've ever done that."

"You never miss?" Jenkins asked.

"No, I said it's nourishment for my spiritual life, and I don't want to miss a meal."

During the conversation, Jenkins remembered looking over Graham's shoulder and spotted the evangelist's open Bible "on the corner of his desk . . . just as he said."

For Graham, praying and reading the Bible weren't optional add-ons; they were core-deep practices. He understood that they were vital to his spiritual health, so he built these rhythms into his life. Prayer and Scripture reading had become ingrained, automatic, as natural as breathing.

HOLY HABITS

It might seem like Scripture doesn't say much about habits. After all most English translations of the Bible contain only one use of the word "habit." In Hebrews 10:25 it says we should "not giv[e] up meeting together, as some are in the habit of doing." But Scripture has plenty to say about practices and patterns of behavior. It urges us to meditate on God's Word "day and night" (Josh. 1:8), confess our sins (James 5:16), pray consistently (Luke 18:1), seek justice (Isa. 1:17), dwell on "whatever is lovely" (Phil. 4:8), "walk humbly" with God (Mic. 6:8), and "speak the truth in love" (Eph. 4:15 NLT). It also contains hundreds of warnings against destructive patterns of action, including the "practice of sinning" (1 John 3:9 NLT), being "conform[ed] to the pattern of this world" (Rom. 12:2), being "drunk on wine" (Eph. 5:18), and being slack in your work (Prov. 18:9). What are these patterns of vice and virtue if not habits?

God also prescribes routines and rituals designed to build holy habits into the lives of His people. The number of routines and rituals in the Old Testament is dizzying. God commanded the ancient Israelites to observe seven sacred annual feasts, keep the Sabbath, tithe their income, purify themselves, worship regularly, and present offerings and sacrifices at the temple. Though the New Testament frees Christians from having to keep the whole Jewish law, there are still sacraments like baptism to symbolize our spiritual rebirth and the communion meal to remind us of the sacrifice of Jesus. On top of this, our weekly gatherings include rituals designed to instill beliefs and behaviors to bring us closer to God and each other.

Even in "low church" settings that don't use the liturgical

calendar or recite ancient creeds, there's often a rather predictable cycle of songs, prayers, and preaching each Sunday. There's Sunday school or midweek small group meetings. These rhythms shouldn't be legalistic duties; at their best, they foster belief and help give individual members much-needed support for the tough task of living the Christian life. These habits are not designed to save us. But as pastor John Starke put it, "There are specific spiritual habits that put us in the way of transformation and change."[14]

A few years ago, I listened to an online talk from a man who gushed about how brilliant the church is to establish such rhythms. He waxed eloquent about singing Christmas carols, looking at religious art and old churches, and the experience of paging through the Bible. The surprising thing about the talk is that the speaker, Alain de Botton, is an atheist. He completely rejects the idea of God and the doctrines of the Christian faith. So why was he praising religion? Because he realized that, by failing to employ the practices of the religious, secular people were failing to make their ideas take hold. "We tend to believe in the modern secular world that if you tell someone something once, they'll remember it. . . . Religions go, 'Nonsense. You need to keep repeating the lesson 10 times a day. So get on your knees and repeat it,'" he said. He wasn't being critical of this insistence on repetition. "Our minds are like sieves," he continued. "So religions are cultures of repetition."[15]

He also celebrated religion's practice of "arrang[ing] time" by means of the calendar. This was a way to ensure adherents "will bump into certain very important ideas" throughout the year. He also extolled how religions "set up rituals" that remind us to do important things as the result of these ideas. He observed that these rituals aren't just mental; they're physical as well. "The other thing that religions know is we're not just brains, we are also bodies. And when they teach us a lesson, they do it via the body."

The point of his lecture was that atheists should start "stealing from religions" to better communicate their ideas and provide a richer experience of life. Though I disagreed with de Botton's atheistic beliefs—and have serious reservations about whether it's possible to tease out religious practices from religious beliefs—I was fascinated by his insights. He made good points. Essentially what he said was that many religious practices are set up to change people and profoundly modify their behavior. They're designed to cultivate habits.

The rhythms you follow as part of a community of faith might seem restrictive or even boring at first. Repeating truths you already know and believe and singing songs you know by heart might seem a little strange, especially to outsiders. But it makes a lot of sense when you understand human nature. Like our atheist friend said, we're sieves. We need to be continually reminded of what's important. We also need repetition if habits are to form around these important beliefs. James K. A. Smith believes that habits aren't manmade tools for improving our behavior; they're how God chooses to shape us.

> We are creatures of habit, that God knows this (since he created us), and thus our gracious, redeeming God meets us where we are by giving us Spirit-empowered, heart-calibrating, habit-forming practices to retrain our loves. This is the means of the Spirit's transformation, not an alternative to Spirit-shaped sanctification.[16]

Ultimately, it's the habits that are built into our lives that shape (for better or worse) who we end up becoming. This is how the prominent nineteenth-century American psychologist William James put it: "All our life so far as it has definite form, is but a mass of habits—practical, emotional, and intellectual—systematically orga- **Habits help us** nized for our weal or woe, and bear- **translate what we** ing us irresistibly toward our destiny, **believe into how we** whatever the latter may be."[17] We're **behave.** not powerless against our habits. In fact, in the next chapter we'll discuss how we can change them. But we ignore their power at our peril. As Christians, forging holy habits is crucial to our spiritual growth. "The goal of the believer," wrote J. I. Packer, "is to become in action what they are in heart." Habits help us translate what we believe into how we behave.

Before brain-imaging studies or double-blind experiments could be conducted, William James understood the power of habit from observing the world around him. But it's important to note that this "mass of habits" that moves us "irresistibly toward our destiny" doesn't happen all at once. Habits start small. They begin with little actions. But over time they snowball. Eventually they change the landscape of our lives. C. S. Lewis wrote about this phenomenon.

> Good and evil both increase at compound interest. That is why the little decisions you and I make every day are of such infinite importance. The smallest good act today is the capture of a strategic point from which, a few months later, you may be able to go on to victories you

never dreamed of. An apparently trivial indulgence in lust or anger today is the loss of a ridge or railway line or bridgehead from which the enemy may launch an attack otherwise impossible.[18]

In the next chapter, we'll explore how we can break bad habits and form good ones. By doing so just maybe we will eliminate the "bridgehead from which the enemy may launch an attack" even as we lay the foundation for "victories you never dreamed of."

Self-Control Training:
Entry #5—Prayer Continued

WELL, IT TURNS OUT I'm not much of a prayer warrior.

I struggle to spend a mere fifteen minutes a day talking to God. And I have a hard time concentrating when I pray. Well, that's an understatement; my mind wanders like a feral cat. Here's a sample of my interior monologue when I try to pray:

Dear Lord, thank You for this day . . . this day . . . man, I'm dreading that 10 a.m. call. Maybe I can reschedule. Speaking of the schedule, are we visiting my parents this weekend? No, that's next weekend. I hope the traffic isn't too bad . . . Oh, right, praying. Lord, I pray for my kids. I thank You for them. Please protect them and . . . my son's been so stubborn lately. Is it just a phase? Maybe I'm too soft on him. I thought I was going to be a strict parent, but I'm a bit of a pushover. Right, right, praying. God, I pray for the missionaries our church sends out. I pray for that family in India . . . I wonder if I could live in India. I love Indian food. Maybe I'd get sick of it though if I had to eat it every day. And it's probably a little different from the Indian food we have over here. But those curries are amazing. I think warmer cultures just have better food, I mean objectively better. Ack! I'm supposed to be praying. Lord, please bless those missionaries in India, eating that delicious Indian food . . .

You get the idea. I have a hard time staying focused when I pray. Sometimes, when my timer goes off, I realize that I've spent most of the time daydreaming. Though I feel like a bit of a failure, I'm going to keep at it. Having a better understanding of how habits work has encouraged me. I know that the early stage of forming a new habit is the hardest. For the first thirty to sixty days, any new routine will feel challenging, even unnatural. But once it becomes a habit, it requires less effort. So, for now, I'll just keep blundering through these prayers. Perhaps over time my concentration will improve.

I also picked up a helpful tip for what to do with my wandering mind. It came from German theologian and Nazi-resister Dietrich Bonhoeffer. During WWII, Hitler closed all the seminaries, so Bonhoeffer ran a secret underground seminary for a small group of men. Bonhoeffer required his students to meditate for two hours each day on a passage of Scripture. But the students were struggling. They came to Bonhoeffer and complained that their minds kept wandering away from the text and back to the troubles at home. "Follow your mind where it goes," Bonhoeffer told them. "Follow it until it stops and then, wherever it stops, make that person or problem a matter for prayer."[19]

I found this strategy liberating. Rather than feeling bad about my wandering mind, or even trying to rein it in—I could follow it. And when I did, I realized Bonhoeffer was right. It often led to people or problems, which I could pray about. It turned out to be a great way to find worthwhile topics to bring to God. Maybe my wandering mind isn't so bad after all.

Chapter 6

Training Your Elephant

Building Healthy Habits into Your Life

"The strength of a man's virtue should not be measured by his special exertions, but by his habitual acts."

—BLAISE PASCAL

Benjamin Franklin had an impressive résumé. When the early American wasn't inventing the lightning rod, bifocal eyeglasses, the odometer, clean-burning stoves, or the flexible urinary catheter (really), he was busy engineering the US postal system, organizing the first fire department, starting the University of Pennsylvania, or writing bestselling books. Oh, and in his spare time he helped found the United States of America. (It's amazing what people got done before Netflix.)

But there was one area in which the famous polymath was a failure: in his attempt to achieve moral perfection. Franklin was twenty when he "conceived the bold and arduous project of arriving at moral perfection" and he tackled the plan with all the vigor and naïveté of youth.[1]

This was the plan. Whenever young Ben faced a moral decision, he resolved to make the right choice. "As I knew, or thought

I knew, what was right or wrong, I did not see why I might not always do the one and avoid the other."[2] In his mind, it was simple. If he knew what was right, he could do what was right . . . every time. Easy peasy. He also sprinkled in a little religion, beseeching the heavens each day to strengthen his efforts. "And conceiving God to be the fountain of wisdom, I thought it right and necessary to solicit His assistance for obtaining it."[3]

Yet Franklin discovered that what seemed simple in theory was anything but in practice. "I soon found I had undertaken a task of more difficulty than I had imagined," he wrote in an understatement for the ages. What was the problem? "While my care was employed in guarding against one fault, I was often surprised by another; habit took the advantage of inattention." In other words, even as he made progress in one area, he lapsed in another. Just as he seemed to be on the cusp of conquering one vice, another would pop up.

Instead of gliding up the mountain of moral perfection, Franklin found himself stuck in the valley, playing an endless game of whack-a-mole with his vices.

Furthermore, he realized that noble intentions were no match for bad habits. "Inclination was sometimes too strong for reason," he concluded. "The mere speculative conviction that it was our interest to be completely virtuous was not sufficient to prevent our slipping."[4]

But Franklin wasn't about to give up. Not that easily. The poster boy for industriousness devised a system to bolster his quest toward moral mastery. First, he settled on thirteen virtues that he wanted to develop in his life: temperance, silence, order, resolution, frugality, industry, sincerity, justice, moderation, cleanliness, tranquility, chastity, and humility.

116

Then he made a chart with the days of the week running horizontally along the top of the page and the virtues running vertically down the left margin. Each time he failed to embody one of the virtues, he would record the indiscretion with a black dot next to the virtue he'd violated.

He also hatched a plan to solve the whack-a-mole problem. Rather than trying to make progress in all thirteen virtues at once, he would tackle them one at a time. "I determined to give a week's strict attention to each of the virtues successively."[5] He hoped that devoting a week to each virtue would allow time for a new habit to solidify before moving on to the next virtue.

Franklin was confident of his new plan. He anticipated having to make fewer and fewer black marks in his "little book." Soon he would have "the encouraging pleasure of seeing on my pages the progress I made in virtue, by clearing successively my lines of their spots, till in the end, by a number of courses, I should be happy in viewing a clean book."[6]

The fine-tuning yielded modest results, but alas, the clean book never materialized. In fact, Franklin recorded so many black marks that big holes began to appear in his little book. He was forced to transfer his charts to a sturdier memorandum book with ivory leaves that he could wipe clean and reuse.

Franklin finally acknowledged the outcome of his audacious quest. "I never arrived at the perfection I had been so ambitious of obtaining, but fell far short of it."[7] Still, Franklin, ever the optimist, was grateful for the meager progress he did make and convinced the experiment yielded innumerable benefits. "I was, by the endeavor, a better and a happier man than I otherwise should have been if I had not attempted it."[8]

Perfection would have to wait for the afterlife. Two years into his bold experiment, he wrote a witty epitaph for his future tombstone, likening his deceased body to a worn-out book that would "appear once more, in a new and more elegant edition, revised and corrected by the Author."[9]

It's easy to laugh at Franklin's naïveté. Did he actually think he could expunge all vices from his life? Most of us would concede that moral perfection is impossible, at least on this side of eternity. If the achievement were possible, the indomitable Benjamin Franklin would be the one to pull it off. But he didn't stand a chance. Franklin started off aiming for perfection, but discovered even modest growth hard to attain. Why did Franklin fail? As we'll see below, Franklin anticipated some key practices of habit formation. As usual, his instincts were prescient. But his actions also betrayed some crucial misunderstandings that sabotaged his success.

INVESTING YOUR WILLPOWER

For me, reading the research on willpower has felt a bit like riding a roller coaster. There were highs, lows, and a few sudden turns. The first dip: discovering that willpower is a finite resource—in other words, that it runs out. Yes, the finding makes sense, but I harbored a belief that if I were just inspired or committed or crazy enough, temptation would always bounce off me like bullets off Superman's chest. But like superhero stories, that notion is pure fiction. Willpower is limited. It runs out, leaving you vulnerable to sin.

Willpower is limited. It runs out, leaving you vulnerable to sin.

Next, the roller coaster lurched up. I discovered that willpower could grow! Just like curling weights gives you bigger biceps, using your willpower makes it stronger over time. Yes, some of us are born with sad and spindly willpower muscles and have to work extra hard to see improvement, but it's possible. It's just a matter of hitting the gym.

But then came another drop: I found that willpower is not enough. The research is clear. It doesn't matter if you are the Arnold Schwarzenegger of willpower, it will be depleted just in the regular course of life. You might hold out a little longer than other people, but you'll run out. That's why we need habits. As we saw in the last chapter, developing good habits preserves your willpower. You rely on instinct and routine rather than conscious effort. Habits make virtuous behavior automatic.

So how does willpower relate to habit?

Imagine someone gave you $1,000 toward your retirement. What should you do with it? One strategy would be to save the money. Put it in in a safe and don't touch it until the day you stop working. The problem is $1,000 isn't much money, not when it comes to funding a retirement. If you managed to save every penny of that money, at best it would fund a few weeks of your retirement. Of course, there's a second strategy: invest it. In a solid investment, that modest sum of money would grow exponentially. When it came time to retire, it could make a significant difference.

That's a good way to think about willpower. It's a relatively small resource, easily exhaustible. It doesn't get us very far. So we need to be strategic about how we use it. We can save it up, which is wise in some instances. But by far the best use of willpower is to use it to initiate healthy patterns of behavior. We need to invest it in good habits.

In a moment we'll look at specific strategies for how to do

that. We'll examine what recent research tells us about how habits function and what we can do to change them. But before we do, let me say a word about how all of this relates to Christian faith. You might read the following strategies and wonder, *What does this have to do with the Bible?*

It's a good question, and I don't want to overstate my case. After all, Christians for centuries got by without a scientific understanding of how habits worked. But I think there are some scriptural principles that encourage us to avail ourselves of this knowledge. The Bible commends forethought and intentionality when it comes to controlling our behavior. We're warned to "make no provision for the flesh" and instructed to "learn to control your own body in a way that is holy and honorable" (1 Thess. 4:4). We're told to "be transformed by the renewing of your mind" (Rom. 12:2), and Scripture is replete with examples of godly characters who took preemptive measures to safeguard themselves against sin (Job 31:1; 1 Cor. 9:27). And, like I wrote in the last chapter, Scripture has tons to say about building holy patterns of action and thought into your life. I see no reason why we shouldn't glean understanding that has come from studying our God-given psychology in order to fulfill these biblical injunctions. Let's look at some of those strategies now.

BEATING PROCRASTINATION

"Diligent hands will rule, but laziness ends in forced labor" (Prov. 12:24).

I'm not sure this verse is about procrastination per se, but it sure feels like it could be. When we're too lazy to tackle important tasks, it usually ends in "forced labor"—stress, scrambling, maybe even pulling an all-nighter to beat a deadline.

So how can we defeat the beast of procrastination? Here are a few tips.

Visit the future. In one study, researchers found that people who are shown digitally aged pictures of themselves put away more money for the future.[10] Why? Because suddenly they are able to visualize (literally) their future selves—and they don't want them to be broke! You can do a similar exercise with whatever tasks you tend to put off. Take an imaginative leap forward and imagine how good you will feel once the task is completed—or how bad you will feel if it isn't. We procrastinate because it gives us pleasure in the short term. Watching Netflix is easier than writing that paper. Slapping the snooze feels better than hitting the treadmill. Doing a little time travel frees you from the tyranny of the present and motivates you to take action today.

Start small. Often we put off projects because we're immobilized by their sheer size and complexity. To overcome this psychological hurdle, figure out a manageable first step and concentrate on that. Try and write a symphony and it will probably never happen. Instead, try writing a few notes. Launching a business is too daunting. But you can start on a business plan. Once you actually begin, you'll be surprised how much progress you make. As with so many things in life, starting is the hardest part. So start small.

Have a little faith. Procrastination is basically a delusion about time. On some level we don't really believe that doing the right thing today will pay off tomorrow. But Scripture is full of reminders that we reap what we sow. Even when we feel like our efforts are futile, we're encouraged to keep going. "Let us not become weary in doing good, for at the proper time we will reap a harvest if we do not give up" (Gal. 6:9). If your goals are righteous and God-honoring, you can rest assured that working hard now will be worth it. So have a little faith. Sow today so you can reap tomorrow. You can beat procrastination.

RIDING ELEPHANTS, LEARNING LOOPS

The psychologist Jonathan Haidt uses a memorable metaphor to explain how we can do this.[11] He likens habit to an elephant, "a strong, tireless animal," and willpower to an elephant rider. An elephant can carry heavy loads great distances. The rider atop the large creature rarely exerts much effort. If the elephant is trained, the rider needs only to push and pull occasionally to send the creature in the desired direction. The elephant does most the work. In the same way, by using our willpower (our conscious effort) to train our habits, we can establish healthy routines that carry us through life.

But how do you train an elephant? It starts with gaining a deeper understanding of the creature.

In the last chapter I provided a bare-bones definition of a habit as action that becomes a pattern of unconscious behavior. But a closer look reveals that every habit has three distinct parts: a cue, a routine, and a reward. The *cue* is a trigger, an external signal that prompts your brain to go into an automatic mode. The cue initiates a *routine*, the behavior you perform. Finally there's the *reward*, some kind of payoff that reinforces the behavior.

The more often you run through this sequence, the more powerful the habit becomes. Soon the cue produces strong emotions, even cravings. Eventually, when you encounter a cue it's almost impossible to resist engaging in the routine to receive the reward. It's a vicious—or virtuous—circle.

THE HABIT LOOP[12]

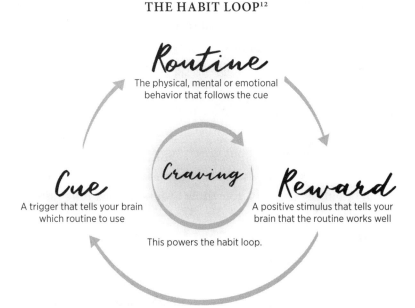

Routine
The physical, mental or emotional
behavior that follows the cue

Cue
A trigger that tells your brain
which routine to use

Craving

Reward
A positive stimulus that tells your
brain that the routine works well

This powers the habit loop.

When I discovered the 3-stage "habit loop," I started to understand my behaviors in a new light. Especially my undesirable behaviors. For instance, like many people, I eat too much when I'm in social situations. When I try a new diet, I usually do well— until I find myself with a group of people. At home, during the week, I can stick to the plan. But then the weekend comes. If I go to a party or out to dinner with friends, my resolve unravels. Suddenly I'm a human garbage disposal. And it happens with very little thought given to the bad choices I'm making. Amid conversations, I consume pizza, chicken wings, French fries, cake, cookies, or whatever's available.

In addition to being unhealthy, it can also be embarrassing. At least for my wife. Recently we attended a fancy fundraiser with catered food. It was held in a sprawling estate, overlooking the city. It was one of the most beautiful houses I'd ever seen. As I made conversation with the other guests, I feasted on beef samosas, bruschetta, and Asian spring rolls. Somewhere during this splurge, I felt someone clutch my arm. It was my wife. "That's your third plate," she whispered. "You might want to slow down."

She was right. I was out of control. Even one of the caterers had made a comment about how hungry I must be. I decided I was done eating for the evening. Yet later in the night, when they brought out the desserts, somehow I found myself filling up another plate.

This experience, and countless others like it, have made me realize that I have a habit of eating poorly in social situations. Understanding the habit loop has helped me break it down. The cue is the social context. What's the routine? Munching like there's no tomorrow. How about the reward? That's a little trickier. It could just be the food. I *do* love food. But that wouldn't explain why I'm able to resist eating poorly at home. Plus (and this is strange) sometimes I don't even enjoy the food I'm eating.

I remember one gathering where I spent the evening grazing on a bowl of mixed crackers that contained hot wasabi peas. I didn't like them, but I kept going back for more. Each time I bit into one of the peas, I grimaced. Yet every few minutes I'd shovel more into my mouth, like a rat coming back for another electric shock. Why? I was curious enough to Google it. I found one study showing that people-pleasers eat more at parties (even when they're not hungry) just to keep pace with the people around them.[13] I'm a people-pleaser extraordinaire, so perhaps that partially explains it.

But I think there's another factor. I've concluded that my habit of eating too much in social contexts is a sort of nervous tic. It alleviates social anxiety. It calms me. It gives me something to do with my hands and my mouth. Take that fancy fundraiser. I was surrounded by strangers. Wealthy strangers. It's intimidating enough to strike up conversations with people you don't know, harder still when they "summer" in the south of France (and you "summer" in the same place that you "winter").

Understanding the habit loop has helped me tackle my bad habit of eating too much in social situations. I can't eliminate this cue from my life (I don't want to become a hermit, even if I'm a skinny one). But now when I'm in a social situation, I try to come in with a plan. Since I know a social context is a cue to eat poorly, I decide beforehand how much I'll allow myself to eat. Another trick I employ is to chew gum. It gives me something to do with my mouth. And since I'd have to spit it out to eat, it's often enough to prevent me from starting.

I'm not the only who has benefited from a greater understanding of how habits work. Studies show that just teaching people about the mechanics of habit has a huge positive impact on their behavior. One series of studies showed the profound impact of teaching exercisers about how habits work. Charles Duhigg wrote about the results in *The New York Times*:

The results were dramatic. Over the next four months, those participants who deliberately identified cues and rewards spent twice as much time exercising as their peers. Other studies have yielded similar results. According to another recent paper, if you want to start running in the morning, it's essential that you choose a simple cue (like always putting on your sneakers before breakfast or leaving your running clothes next to your bed) and a clear reward (like a midday treat or even the sense of accomplishment that comes from ritually recording your miles in a log book). After a while, your brain will start anticipating that reward—craving the treat or the feeling of accomplishment—and there will be a measurable neurological impulse to lace up your jogging shoes each morning.[14]

Duhigg's conclusion: "simply understanding how habits work makes them easier to control."[15] Equipped with this knowledge, the exercisers could think strategically about using cues and rewards to reinforce their exercise routine. To borrow Haidt's language, understanding the elephant made them better riders.

CREATE HABITS ONE AT A TIME

Every year millions of Americans (including me) make New Year's resolutions. Of course, just as predictably as these resolutions are made, they're broken. By February, 80 percent of us have stopped jogging, started sleeping in, or jumped headfirst back into whatever old habits we promised to break. Within mere weeks, that list we conceived in a burst of optimism becomes a quiet source of shame. Twelve months after making our resolutions, only 8 percent of us have stuck with them. Why?

Well, the first problem is that we tend to make New Year's

resolutions (plural). A New Year's resolution would stand a chance at sticking; resolutions, however, have nearly no chance. It goes back to our conversation about willpower. Like we've seen, once a habit is established it takes very little effort to keep it going. Just tug the elephant's ear occasionally, and the large animal keeps lumbering along. But that's not true of initiating a new habit. Forming a new habit (especially a good habit) is a tremendous draw on your willpower reserves. Initially the new behavior may be physically or mentally challenging. It will cut against the grain of your natural inclinations. It takes effort. Lots of it. Multiply that output of effort by three or four or five, like we often do with New Year's resolutions, and you're almost guaranteed to fail. It's like trying to climb a mountain—with someone on your back.

Remember Benjamin Franklin's audacious goal to achieve moral perfection? That might sound like one goal, but it wasn't. He identified thirteen different practices he wanted to master. Thirteen! No wonder he found it "a task of more difficulty than [he] had imagined." Striving for perfection in thirteen areas of moral behavior all at once overtaxed even Franklin's prodigious will. The upshot was that he failed to make much progress in any of them. Only once he corrected his mistake, and opted to focus on one at a time, did he begin to make some headway.

We'd be wise to do the same. If you're trying to build new habits in your life, introduce them one at a time. Don't start a diet the same day you begin running. Don't launch a new Bible reading program the same day you resolve to start praying every morning. This may feel counterintuitive. There are defining moments in life when we want to reset and change everything. In our zeal to begin fresh, we resolve to change all kinds of behaviors at once. Unfortunately, our enthusiasm to make sweeping changes guarantees we'll fail to make any. So rather than trying to create multiple habits at once, focus on creating one habit at a time. Once you've established one healthy habit, then use your replenished willpower to move on and create another.

NUDGE YOURSELF TO BETTER CHOICES

We like to think that our actions are based purely on free will. But as we've already seen, friends, habits, and energy levels all influence our decisions. There's another factor to consider—the choices available to us. The options we're presented with play a powerful role in determining our behavior.

Arranging options to encourage healthy or virtuous decisions is what economists Richard H. Thaler and Cass R. Sunstein call "choice architecture."[16] For example, studies have shown that the number of organ donors doubles when people are asked to opt out of being a donor rather than opting in. The way the choice is presented has a dramatic impact on how people respond. Choice architecture is all around us, and it doesn't always work in our favor. When you walk into a grocery store, you encounter the produce section first. That's by design. The owners know that once you put some asparagus in your cart, you'll give yourself permission to pick up Oreos when you hit Aisle 7.

I became something of a choice architect when I had children. "You can eat your broccoli and stay up for another hour, or you can skip it and go to bed right now," I announce to my kids. I don't mention that I was going to let them stay up for another hour anyway, but suddenly they're cramming broccoli into their mouths. Choice architecture strikes again.

Thaler and Sunstein note that when people are presented with a range of choices, they will usually take the path of least resistance. The key then is to rig the system in favor of healthy behaviors. They advocate for "nudging" people toward better conduct by limiting their options and making good choices easier.

While Thaler and Sunstein apply the concept of choice architecture to governments and corporations, there's no reason we can't use it in our personal lives. So become your own choice architect. Think through the choices you're giving yourself every day. Does the food in your cupboard encourage healthy eating? Even if you have healthy food in your house, if it takes longer to prepare, you'll probably opt for quicker, less healthy options. What about exercise? Does your preferred mode of physical activity require a lot of equipment and a drive across town? If so, you'll usually stay on the couch.

Think through your spiritual habits too. If you give yourself an option of scrolling through Facebook or reading your Bible, you'll probably choose the former. It's not necessarily because you're unspiritual; it's just that reading your friends' updates is easier than reading Scripture. So keep your phone out of your room and put your Bible beside your bed. By arranging your choices to support better decisions, you'll find your behavior improves. It takes a little effort and forethought to arrange the choices you encounter every day, but it's worth it. Your future self will thank you.

SWAP AND START SMALL

"A nail is driven out by another nail. Habit is overcome by habit," wrote the sixteenth-century theologian Desiderius Erasmus. Five centuries later we understand just how right he was. Study after study has demonstrated the wisdom of starting a new habit by replacing an old one. By doing this, you essentially get a two-for-one deal: you lose a bad habit, while gaining a good one. Smokers, for instance, are very unlikely to quit if they don't find some replacement behavior to smoking. "You can't extinguish a bad habit, you can only change it," Duhigg writes. And the way to change it is to perform a sort of surgery on the loop of the bad habit. "To change a habit, you must keep the old cue, and deliver the old reward, but insert a new routine."[17]

When trying to establish a new, healthy habit, start small. If you try to do too much on Day One you'll drain your willpower and fail to repeat the behavior the next day. And without repetition, new habits can't take hold. Remember: at the outset, you're trying to trick your brain into forming a new habit. Psychologists refer to this approach as forming "tiny" or "micro" habits. It's a tactic to use the habit loop to create a pattern of behavior that you can build on.

Say you want to start running every morning. Begin by identifying a cue: maybe it's drinking a health shake or seeing your running shoes at the front door. Then perform the routine in a way that doesn't demand exerting too much effort. Perhaps it's just walking around the block once. Or it could be even smaller: put your shoes on and jog in place for thirty seconds. When you finish, give yourself a reward. It could be a cup of coffee, a piece of chocolate, or a few minutes watching TV.

At first, it might feel silly to reward yourself for completing such a small task. But remember, you're conditioning your brain. When you see those shoes by the door, your brain will expect exercise. As you exercise, it will begin anticipating a reward. As you move through this habit loop repeatedly—cue, routine, reward—the behavior will become cemented into your life, and you can gradually increase the intensity of your workouts. Soon you'll head out to run every morning without even thinking about it.

Another cardinal rule of habit formation: be consistent. Don't run first thing in the morning one day, and go for an evening jog the next. Pick a time and try to stick with it. If you're trying to read your Bible every day, try to do it at the same time, in the same room, in the same chair. When it comes to making a habit stick, familiarity is key. I'm not suggesting you slog through new practices—especially spiritual ones—without feeling or passion. But you're far more likely to stick with the new behavior through the crucial habit-forming window if you keep the conditions the same.

PUT IN THE TIME

How long does it take to form a habit? The most common answer is twenty-one days. At least that's the number that gets bandied about in advice columns, blog posts, and TV shows. In truth, the twenty-one-day guideline only works for very simple tasks. If it's something more difficult or complex, research shows that three weeks is probably too optimistic. One large study found the average number of days it took for participants to reach "automaticity" (scientific speak for when behavior becomes habitual) was an average of sixty-six days.[18]

As you can see, habits aren't developed overnight. It takes at least a month or two of concerted effort to continue performing a certain behavior before it becomes second nature. When Franklin realized it was too difficult to tackle all thirteen virtues at one time, he decided to tackle them one by one. Like I mentioned, in light of what we know today about habits, that was a wise move. Unfortunately, he gave himself only one week to focus on a virtue before moving on to the next one. That's not even close to enough time to firm up a habit.

Not only that, but his efforts to perfectly embody a virtue were too lofty and undefined. Rather than trying to achieve justice, he would have been better off identifying practices he could regularly do to become more just. Instead of vaguely aiming for "frugality," he should have made a budget. Now I'm being awfully hard on a guy who accomplished more than I could in ten lifetimes. But that's kind of the point: I don't have the willpower of a Ben Franklin. And that means I'm going to have to rely on habit.

When I look back at many of my attempts to get healthier or practice a spiritual discipline, I'm struck by how often I've given up after a week or two. Often we don't even realize how close we come to that magical threshold where the behavior becomes second nature. Now, when I'm trying to create a new habit, I'm conscious of pushing through to that point. It's encouraging to know that the behavior will become more automatic as I go, demanding less and less effort over time. I try to remember pastor John Ortberg's words on why we struggle to form holy habits: "Construction today. Freedom tomorrow."[19]

SPIRITUAL KEYSTONES

Not all habits are created equal. Some habits, in addition to changing one behavior, encourage better behavior in other areas of your life as well. Researchers call them *keystone habits*, and they have a synergistic effect. They "shift, dislodge and remake other patterns," making additional healthy habits more likely to form.[20]

Exercise is a well-known keystone habit. When people start exercising regularly, they also have more patience, less stress, and become more productive at work. Having family dinners is another keystone habit. Studies have shown that when families observe the increasingly rare ritual of gathering to eat together, their children's emotional control and performance at school improves.[21]

What about spiritual keystone habits? There are at least three spiritual practices that qualify: prayer, Bible reading, church attendance.

Dozens of studies have pointed toward the positive impact of prayer. According to an article summarizing the research in *Psychology Today*, praying regularly makes you nicer, more forgiving, more trusting, and offsets the negative health effects of stress. In addition, prayer has shown to boost self-control. And, as we saw earlier, it's one of the only behaviors proven to counteract ego depletion. No wonder it exerts such a powerful influence on other areas of life. One church leader identified prayer as a keystone habit in his life. Listen to how he described the differences he saw.

I had always prayed, but life often got so busy that it was difficult to keep a consistent practice. It wasn't a habit. About 10 years ago, I made a commitment to make prayer the first thing I do every day. It took a few months of doing this regularly before it became a habit. But once it did, the rest, as they say, is history.

Over the last decade, a series of habits have "cascaded" from the keystone habit of prayer. These include exercise, meditation, journaling and fasting. They didn't happen all at once. Each time, I would feel led to apply my focus and effort to a particular practice. Over the course of time, that practice would become a habit. My own experience is that each time it gets a little bit easier to develop a new habit.[22]

For him, the practice of prayer triggered the creation of other spiritual habits.

Bible reading also pays huge dividends for people across the spiritual spectrum. Just how important is Scripture engagement? Greg Hawkins and Cally Parkinson did a landmark study of the spiritual growth over more than 250,000 people in 1,000 churches. This was their conclusion about the impact of Scripture engagement:

Nothing has a greater impact on spiritual growth than reflection on Scripture. If churches could do only one thing to help people at all levels of spiritual maturity grow in their relationship with Christ, their choice is clear. They would inspire, encourage, and equip their people to read the Bible—specifically, to reflect on Scripture for meaning in their lives. . . .

Bible-engagement is the single most spiritually catalytic activity a person can engage in.[23]

The fact that Bible reading is a keystone habit should come as no surprise. After all, God gives us His Word as a primary means of transformation. Meditating on Scripture keeps us from sin (Ps. 119:1), gives us direction (119:105), and trains us in righteousness (2 Tim. 3:16). John Stott said, "We must allow the Word of

God to confront us, to disturb our security, to undermine our complacency and to overthrow our patterns of thought and behavior."[24] In other words, the Bible should correct us, then completely overhaul our habits.

Church attendance is another powerful keystone habit. A 2016 Harvard study found that women who attended religious services frequently were one-third less likely to die over a twenty-year period. No surprise, you might think. Churchgoers are less likely to smoke or abuse drugs and alcohol. But it wasn't healthier lifestyles that made the difference. The researchers adjusted for those factors, and still saw the dramatic difference.

Even occasional church-attenders reaped benefits. They were 13 percent less likely to die over the twenty-year period as their nonattending counterparts. Tyler VanderWeele, a professor of epidemiology at the Harvard T.H. Chan School of Public Health, concluded, "Service attendance may be a powerful and underappreciated health resource."[25] In a USA Today column, VanderWeele was less circumspect, proclaiming, "Religion may be a miracle drug."[26]

Other studies have identified specific health effects associated with church attendance. They've found that churchgoing boosts your immune system, decreases blood pressure, and lowers your cholesterol. "One of the most striking scientific discoveries about religion in recent years," writes T. M. Luhrmann, a professor of anthropology at Stanford, "is that going to church weekly is good for you."[27] And the health benefits are just the tip of the iceberg. Studies show that churchgoers are less prone to mental illness, report higher levels of happiness, and have better sex lives. Young people who attend are less likely to smoke, abuse drugs and alcohol, or commit violent crimes. They have higher GPAs and are less likely to live in poverty. They're even more likely to wear seat belts.[28]

Church attendance is so powerful because it includes the other two spiritual keystone habits. Author David Mathis sums it up.

> The reason corporate worship may be the single most important Christian habit, and our greatest weapon in the fight for joy, is because like no other single habit, corporate worship combines all three essential principles of God's ongoing supply of grace for the Christian life: hearing his voice (in his word), having his ear (in prayer), and belonging to his body (in the fellowship of the church).[29]

The research shows that prayer, Bible reading, and church attendance all have extrinsic benefits, making us more likely to engage in healthier patterns in all areas of life. But as believers, we know they have intrinsic value; we do them to grow closer to God and each other.

NO SHORTCUTS

Habits are hard. They're not shortcuts or life hacks. Yes, eventually they enable us to live better lives without exhausting our willpower, but they start with a burst of effort. Our brains are lazy. Our wills are weak. Our nature is bent. Even if we employ all the approaches outlined above, it still takes sweat and struggle and striving to break the inertia of your old ways of doing things and move in a new direction. Author Mike Cosper describes this incremental nature of how Christians change.

> There are no magic pills. There are no shortcuts. Discipleship is like any other good thing that's worth doing, be it learning a language, learning an instrument, or getting in shape; we grow as disciples in small steps, a day at a time, over months and years.[30]

Cosper is right to connect habits with discipleship. It's no coincidence that *discipleship* and *discipline* are linguistically related. It takes hard work, discipline, to free ourselves of sinful habits and replace them with righteous ones. Thankfully, we don't have to do it on our own. We don't have to be Ben Franklins, armed with a towering intellect and ironclad resolve in order to make progress. God is there, willing to reward our modest attempts to change. He actually enables and empowers us along the way.

The broadcaster and cleric Richard Holloway describes the divine assistance that meets our paltry efforts: "God is waiting eagerly to respond with new strength to each little act of self-control, small disciplines of prayer, feeble searching after him."[31]

Habits aren't everything. As pastor and author Darryl Dash writes, "It's possible to build great habits and completely miss the point, which is ongoing spiritual growth and intimacy with God."[32] Rather, as Dash goes on to explain, habits are a means to an end. "The point [of habits], in the end, is our pursuit of God. We need habits that support that pursuit. We won't pursue God without them. They are ways of putting ourselves in the path of God's grace."[33]

Self-Control Training:
Entry #6—Fasting

I HAVE A BAD HISTORY WITH FASTING.

It started in my teens. When I was sixteen, I signed up for a 30-Hour Famine, an event designed to raise funds for hungry children while giving comfy Western kids a small taste of deprivation. It now strikes me as more than a little insensitive to describe a mere day and a half without food, while playing games in a church gymnasium, as a "famine," but I was in.

We were instructed to start fasting at 9:00 p.m. the night before. The next day we just had to skip breakfast and lunch, then head to the church around 7:00 p.m. We'd play games all evening and break the fast with a giant pizza party at 3:00 a.m.

My buddy Dan agreed to do it with me. We hung out on the day of the fast for moral support. But we made the mistake of talking about food. A lot. I think it was Dan's vivid description of the perfect bacon cheeseburger that ultimately caused our downfall. On the way to the church, we stopped off at local restaurant where our resolve died in a heap of burgers and chicken wings. We never even made it to the church. We'd held out for twenty-one hours. And for eight of those hours, we'd been asleep.

Fast forward ten years, and I was signing up for another fast, this time with my wife. It was the voguish "Daniel fast," inspired by the biblical Daniel's decision to subsist on veggies rather than eat the "royal foods," like wine, bread, and meat sacrificed to idols, offered to him and his fellow exiles by King Nebuchadnezzar. After a few miserable days of a vegetable diet, my wife and I dragged ourselves to a midweek Bible study. We were hoping for some inspiration or at least the chance to commiserate. The pastor, who was leading the study, seemed suspiciously chipper. Midway through the study, he casually unveiled a bagel and started munching.

"I'm not going to lie," he chuckled. "It's been hard not putting anything on these bagels."

I felt betrayed. "Bagels?" I whispered to my wife. "Bagels aren't part of the Daniel fast! Don't tell me they had bagels in Babylon!" That was just the excuse I needed. That night, I ate all the royal foods I could think of—minus the meat sacrificed to pagan idols. Fasting fail #2.

Throughout the years, I've tried to fast a few other times, always with mixed results. Some people wax eloquent about the clarity and piercing spiritual insights fasting brings, but my experience has been more like a miserable fog. It's something I dread. The bad breath, the grumpiness, the lightheadedness. Yet I still think it's an important spiritual discipline—one I want to start practicing, if only occasionally. This time, I decided to go solo. Given my track record of fasting with others, that seemed to make sense. And my first attempt would be nothing fancy, just a twenty-four-hours with nothing but water. It shouldn't be a problem.

Chapter 7

Grace Means I Don't Need Self-Control

... And Other Dumb Things Christians Think

"If we know that the aim of the Holy Spirit is to lead man to the place of self-control, we shall not fall into passivity but shall make good progress in spiritual life. 'The fruit of the Spirit is self-control.'"

—WATCHMAN NEE

When I think of why I'm a Christian, it really boils down to one word: grace.

As a teenager, I read through the Gospels and fell in love with the person of Jesus. It wasn't just His miracles and teaching that impressed me. It was how He treated people, especially those people society mistreated or neglected: the way He defended a woman about to be stoned for adultery; the way He sought out a hated tax collector; the way He cut through a crowd to reach a blind man crying out for help on the side of the road. Jesus was constantly seeking out the unloved and lowly to offer forgiveness, healing, friendship, and love.

As I read those stories I was moved. Somehow, in the fog of my adolescent insecurity, I realized that the same grace on display in the Gospels extended to me. I've never recovered.

I'm far from alone. Glimpsing God's undeserved favor has changed the hearts of millions. Grace woos and softens, draws and transforms. It famously changed the heart of one cruel slave trader who marveled at "amazing grace that saved a wretch like me." C. S. Lewis was once asked what separated Christianity from all other religions. "Oh, that's easy," he said, "grace." While most religions possess some karmic system to show how hard you have to work to win God's favor, grace gives it away for free. In fact, that's the essential characteristic of grace: it's free, a gift. It's no coincidence that the word *gratis* is derived from grace. That's what makes grace so amazing. You just accept it. No striving required.

CAN'T I JUST "LET GO AND LET GOD"?

But this beautiful quality presents a bit of a puzzle when it comes to self-control. If grace is free, shouldn't holiness be free too? Why should I have to exert effort to live a disciplined, righteous life? Won't God just *give* me sinless behavior, no self-control required?

Some people think so.

When I mentioned the topic of this book on social media, one friend took exception. "Self-control is the wrong concept," he wrote. "I can never control myself. I can only surrender control to a higher power, but I will never have control over myself. Not in this life."

I could dismiss his opinion as extreme, but I've heard similar sentiments from many others. In fact there have been whole movements in church history defined by their belief that we progress in the Christian life only as passive recipients.[1] And the legacy of these movements is alive and well today. The key to rising above temptation isn't to resist or struggle, they say. All you have to do is "let go and let God!" In fact, if you're struggling, that's proof-positive you're doing something wrong. It means you must be trying too hard.

Obviously, I disagree with this idea. If I didn't, it would be pretty weird to write a book about self-control. But I have to admit, passive transformation sounds wonderful to me. It's probably just because I'm naturally lazy. I'm always looking for a shortcut or cheat sheet, especially when it comes to doing hard things. I'd love to progress in my spiritual life without exerting effort. Throw up my feet, put on some good music, and let the changing begin. Jesus, take the wheel!

Sadly, for lazy me, I don't find this idea in Scripture. Instead I see exhortations to resist temptation, die to sin, deny self, fight the good fight, and strive for godliness. The Greek word in our Bibles that we translate as "strive" is *agonizomai*, implying an intense, purposeful struggle. It comes from *agónia* (the lexical root of "agony"). It's the same word the gospel writers use to describe Jesus' inner turmoil on the eve of His crucifixion. That hardly sounds like passivity to me.

Yet I've found that words like *struggle* or *strive* seem to be off-limits in Christian circles. If you don't believe me, just use them around your Christians friends and see how they react. If you say something like, "I've really been striving in my spiritual life lately," your statement will likely elicit concern or sympathy. A well-meaning friend might comfort or correct you with some variation of the "let go and let God" cliché.

We weren't always uncomfortable with the language of

striving. Listen to these words from a sermon Billy Graham preached in 1957:

> The Christian is likened to a boxer, who masters his own body and practices self restraint, and all the way through the New Testament you'll read words like this, describing the Christian life: Fight, wrestle, run, work, suffer, endure, resist, agonize, persevere. All of these are New Testament words describing the Christian life. It is to be a disciplined life.[2]

I find such descriptions of the Christian life jarring, probably because I've grown so accustomed to equating spirituality with passivity. But there's no getting around it: they're thoroughly biblical. And taking them seriously will mean resetting my expectations. I can't expect my life to be a pleasure cruise toward holiness. I'll have to come to peace with the difficult truth that growth won't always feel good. In fact, like an athlete pushing his body to the breaking point, I'm learning that progress can feel a lot like pain.

BUT WHAT ABOUT GRACE?

If this teaching is so clear in Scripture, why do we shy away from it? Part of it is just laziness. I know my reluctance is largely a smokescreen, a way of avoiding the humbling, hard work of seeking to change. But there is another reason why we're uneasy with the idea of striving, and it comes from a good place. We want to protect grace.

The Christian experience can be divided into two major categories: *justification* and *sanctification*. Justification means we're made right before God. This is what happens when God saves us. When we put our trust in Christ, we cross from death to life and become members of God's family. This astonishing event happens purely by the grace of God. We don't deserve it. We can't earn it. We can't start delivering pizzas at night to pay God back. It happens instantaneously, even if we can't recall exactly when it occurred. God, in His infinite mercy, reaches down and saves us. We're justified.

Sanctification is different. It refers to the spiritual growth that happens after you're saved. It's about becoming more and more like Jesus. Like justification, it is initiated and empowered by God. But unlike justification, it happens gradually, over a lifetime. It's a process. And it demands human effort. As my friend Matt Capps says, "Salvation is surrender. Sanctification is war."

The problem is that we tend to conflate these categories. We want to protect the beautiful truth that we're saved by grace alone and not by anything we've done. So we carry that truth over and apply it to sanctification. When we do that, we assume sanctification should happen like salvation: instantaneously and without effort. But in our attempt to protect one biblical truth, we distort another. We end up believing sanctification is a passive enterprise in which God transforms us unilaterally. But as we've seen, this isn't a biblical idea, and it hampers our spiritual progress. As pastor Kevin DeYoung writes, "Some Christians are stalled out in their sanctification for simple lack of effort."[3]

Furthermore, viewing sanctification in this way does nothing to protect our understanding of justification as a gift from God. Again DeYoung writes, "Stressing the necessity of personal holiness should not undermine in any way our confidence in justification by faith alone."[4] In fact if you try to eliminate the need for holiness, you wind up with what Dietrich Bonhoeffer called "cheap grace," an unbiblical view of the gospel that embraces Christ's message but refuses the hard work of following Him. Such an approach devalues grace and cripples our spiritual growth. But by striving for holiness, we honor the gift of grace.

ISN'T STRIVING LEGALISM?

At this point, objections might be popping up in your mind.

Are you saying God doesn't play a role in my spiritual growth? That I can just roll up my sleeves, and transform all by myself? Isn't that legalism?

In his book on spiritual disciplines, pastor John Ortberg addresses this common reaction. "People who live under the bondage of legalism and then hear the message of grace are sometimes leery that talk of disciplines might lead to another form of religious oppression," he writes. Yet he assures readers that "spiritual disciplines don't oppose or live in tension with grace." Rather, they complement each other.[5] If you're worried I'm making the case for backbreaking legalism, let me put your mind at ease: I'm not. Guarding against passivity is crucial. But we need to avoid the opposite, and equally dangerous, error: thinking we can transform all by ourselves. Let me be clear: true spiritual growth doesn't come apart from God's empowerment. You can't pull your soul up by your spiritual bootstraps. If you try, you'll become like the Pharisees. You will end up trusting in your own efforts to fulfill God's law, never quite sure whether you've done enough.

So we need to guard against passivity and exert effort. On the other hand, we must draw on God's power to live the Christian life. Fudging on either commitment will stall our spiritual growth.

Discounting our role in sanctification leads to license. Ignoring God's role leads to legalism.

But here's good news: there's really no conflict between divine empowerment and human effort. As the late Dallas Willard said, "Grace is not opposed to effort. It is opposed to earning."[6] The Bible is crammed with passages showing both the divine and human role in sanctification.

Consider this passage from Romans: "if by the Spirit you put to death the misdeeds of the body, you will live" (8:13). Note the dual roles represented in this verse. Who is the active agent here? Well, "*you* put to death the misdeeds of the body." Does that mean God isn't involved? Not at all! The passage is equally clear that this crucial act of killing sin only happens "by the *Spirit*." We need the Spirit to eradicate sin in our lives.

In 2 Peter 1:3 we see the same pattern: "His divine power has given us everything we need for a godly life through our knowledge of him who called us by his own glory and goodness." At first blush, it appears we are mere passengers on the train to holiness. After all, God has provided the power . . . what's left for us to do? A lot, apparently. The passage goes on to command us, "For this very reason, make every effort to add to your faith goodness; and to goodness, knowledge; and to knowledge self-control." Did you catch that? We're commanded to "make every effort" *because* "His divine power has given us everything we need for a godly life." For Peter, divine empowerment and human effort aren't enemies. They're allies. God has given us His power. That's why we strive.

Divine empowerment and human effort aren't enemies. They're allies. God has given us His power. That's why we strive.

In Philippians 2:12 we're commanded to "work out your salvation with fear and trembling." That language clearly shows the requirement of human effort. But the very next verse reminds us of who is really effecting the change: "for it is God who works in you to will and to act in order to fulfill his good purpose" (2:13).

Perhaps the clearest example of the divine and human roles operating in tandem comes from Colossians 1:29: "For this *I toil*, struggling with all his energy that *he* [Jesus] powerfully works within me" (ESV, emphasis mine). Here there's no doubt that Paul is expending effort. Another translation reads, "I strenuously contend." At the same time, it is equally clear that it is "he" (Jesus) who is working within him. And it's Jesus' internal working that motivates Paul's effort: "For this I toil . . ." These passages (and scores of others) show that divine empowerment and human effort are not only compatible, they're complementary. We may be tempted to pit them against each other, but it appears that the writers of Scripture envisioned them working together. Perhaps that's why theologians call our spiritual activities—prayer, Bible reading, service—"means of grace." They're ways that we cooperate with God's supernatural work in our lives.

I used to work for a company that didn't offer retirement benefits. I had the option to contribute to a 401(k), but my employer didn't have a matching program. Guess what? I didn't put in a dime. But then I started working for a company that had a program that matched my retirement contributions. In fact, they did more than match. They doubled them! Guess who started investing? Every month I put in the maximum possible contribution. Knowing that each dollar I put in was doubled motivated me. Sure, it was still a sacrifice to have a few hundred bucks shaved off each paycheck, but it was well worth it.

That's a very flawed analogy for Spirit-empowered striving. But it gets one part of it right. When I know that God's power is available, it makes me more likely to strive, not less. The promise of His supernatural assistance motivates me to participate. I like the way Todd Hunter puts it: "Sin always brings a struggle. But rather than struggling against the Spirit and our conscience, we need to strive *with* them."[7]

That's not to say that our efforts are on equal footing with God's power. If you're tempted to give your effort too much credit, remember this: God is the one who gives you the desire to strive after holiness in the first place! He's also the one who alerts you to the presence of sin, helps you discern what's right, and then empowers your efforts to do it! And when you fail, as we all do, He's there to offer forgiveness and restoration. It begins and ends with God. Yes, He allows us to contribute to the process, but we should never mistake our modest part in the play as the leading role. When it comes to spiritual growth, God does the heavy lifting.

And thank God for that! We need His power! I don't know if you've noticed, but the Christian life is hard. Have you read the Sermon on the Mount? How in the world am I supposed to rejoice when people persecute me? Or love my enemies? Or not lust (even in my heart)? If I'm relying only on my own efforts, I don't stand a chance. Obeying God's commands is impossible apart from God's strength. But we still have to obey.

Sanctification is like sailing. Sailors can't move without the wind, but that doesn't mean they kick up their feet on the deck and wait to start moving. They're tying knots, adjusting sails, turning the rudder—all while making sure the boom doesn't swing across the deck and smack them in the head. Sailing is hardly a passive enterprise—but it's completely dependent upon the wind. In a similar way, we're completely dependent on God's Spirit to make progress. But we're not passive. Our effort works with God's power to move us forward. I remember talking about the tension with a friend, Kim Cummings. She was grappling with the relationship between God's empowerment and human effort, and came to this conclusion: "I participate in this work, this sanctification, through prayer, obedience, interaction with God's Word and His saints. But ultimately the work is His and I can rest in that."

And what about grace? Well, it's still beautifully, wondrously, irrevocably free. We don't add anything to it, and we can't take anything away. Striving after holiness is just the appropriate response to the lavish gift of salvation. We're not trying to earn what's been given. Instead we act out of gratitude and joy. And that leads to effort. "You have never seen people more active," Dallas Willard said, "than those who have been set on fire by the grace of God."[8]

THE POWER OF A FRESH START

Grace is instrumental in salvation. It also spurs us to righteous behavior. Scripture tells us that it is "the grace of God" that "teaches us to say 'No' to ungodliness and worldly passions, and to live self-controlled, upright and godly lives" (Titus 2:11–12).

The idea that grace teaches self-control can seem a bit surprising. After all, if I'm freely forgiven of my sins by the grace of God, why resist sin? If there's always more forgiveness on tap, why strive after righteousness? The apostle Paul anticipated this reaction— "Shall we go on sinning so that grace may increase?"—and immediately shot it down: "By no means!" he wrote. "We are those who have died to sin; how can we live in it any longer?" (Rom. 6:1–2)

To Paul, the idea that we should keep sinning because of grace was silly, absurd, the equivalent of Bill Gates knocking off a 7-Eleven. Instead, forgiveness lays the groundwork for transformation.

In high school I had a close friend who described himself as an atheist. When he told me he didn't believe in God, I could only think of one biblical rejoinder: "The fool says in his heart 'There is no God'" (Ps. 14:1). Since he was a lot stronger than me, and liked to fight, I kept the verse to myself.

I tried talking to him about my faith, but nothing seemed to get through to him. Nothing except for this: I described to him, as best I could, the experience of forgiveness. "There's nothing like coming to God with all the bad things you've done and asking for Him to cleanse you," I told him. "It's like taking a shower after being dirty for a long time. You feel completely new, totally clean."

He was silent.

"Hey, man. I don't mean to preach at you," I said.

"That doesn't sound like preaching," he replied looking off at something. "It doesn't sound like preaching at all."

I wasn't much of an evangelist, but I got one thing right. There's something powerful about the prospect of forgiveness, of being made clean. As the Presbyterian minister Henry Van Dyke said, "For love is but the heart's immortal thirst to be completely known and all forgiven." When you feel that forgiveness, the last thing you want to do is rush out and start sinning.

In 1 Corinthians 6, Paul gives a long list of "wrongdoers" who will not inherit the kingdom of God. The list includes some pretty despicable characters, including swindlers, drunks, thieves, and adulterers. But before his readers could feel too superior, he added these words, " . . . and that is what some of you were."

Those descriptions only applied to his readers in the past tense. Something had changed: "you were washed, you were sanctified" (6:11), Paul reminded them. In other words, because of the fact that they'd been forgiven, they had entered a whole new way of living. The next verses unpack how "washed" people are to live, by "not [being] mastered by anything" and living free from sexual immorality. Holiness flows from forgiveness.

It's a spiritual principle, and a psychological one. Researchers talk about the benefits of the "fresh start effect." Basically it means that when we feel like we've been given a clean slate, our behavior improves. That helps explain why people who use "temporal landmarks" like birthdays, the beginning of a new year, or even the beginning of the week to start pursuing a new goal make greater progress. They feel like they've been given a new start and they don't want to mess it up. According to Francesca Gino, a behavioral scientist, "We feel more motivated and empowered to work hard toward reaching our goals when we feel like our past failures are behind us."[9]

That's good news for Christians. We get the ultimate blank slate when we place our faith in Christ. Then we receive that blank slate over and over again. First when we come to Christ and receive a whole new life (2 Cor. 5:17), and then repeatedly as we repent of our sins and ask God for forgiveness (1 John 1:9).

Unfortunately, we don't always take advantage of this blank slate. Or at least I don't. When I mess up, I'm reluctant to confess my sins and ask God for forgiveness. Not only that, but I start avoiding my Bible and stop praying. In order words, I start avoiding God (as if I could).

I realize this makes no sense. I know God loves me unconditionally. But because of my actions, suddenly I feel like we're not on talking terms. This strange avoidance behavior is always a mistake. When I fail to confess my sins, I'm more likely to sin again. *What's one more sin*, I think. *I'm already messing up.*

Researchers have a name for this phenomenon too. They call it the "What-The-Hell Effect." Basically, it means that after messing up, we tend to mess up even more. It was coined by dieting researchers who noticed that when their subjects had even small indiscretions (a bite of ice cream or one slice of pizza) it was followed by a full-on binge. Psychologist Kelly McGonigal explains this thinking behind this behavior.

> Giving in makes you feel bad about yourself, which motivates you to do something to feel better. And what's the cheapest, fastest strategy for feeling better? Often the very thing you feel bad about. . . . It's not the first giving-in that guarantees the bigger relapse. It's the feelings of shame, guilt, loss of control and loss of hope that follow the first relapse.[10]

I'm convinced this dynamic plagues my spiritual life as well. When I sin, the shame and guilt drive me away from God. I feel bad about myself, and in a cruel irony, I engage in more of the sin that made me feel bad in the first place.

When I confess my sins, the circle stops. I feel like I've hit the refresh button on my spiritual life. Suddenly I'm motivated

It can be natural to think that feeling really bad about yourself is the way to improve your behavior. But piling on guilt is never the answer. It's to keep diving back into grace.

to resist sin and pursue holiness. Wallowing in my guilt merely makes me sin more. Confession gives me a fresh start and I don't want to mess it up. It can be natural to think that feeling really bad about yourself is the way to improve your behavior. But piling on guilt is never the answer. It's to keep diving back into grace.

THE POWER OF ATTACHMENT

There's another, even more profound way that grace enables self-control. It provides the deep trust in God's goodness that's essential to live a righteous life. Without grace, you're always left wondering where you stand with God. You're never sure if God loves you, whether God is *for* you. You might think such uncertainty would spur you to greater action. (After all, you're never quite sure if you've done enough.) Yet it doesn't. It fuels resignation and defeat. It engenders distrust in God and drains your ability to please Him.

If you've taken Psychology 101, you've probably heard about attachment theory. The theory gained traction in the 1960s when researchers had parents do what my wife and I do every Sunday morning: leave their young children in a room with strangers. The difference is that the researchers stuck around to observe how the children reacted.

Some of the babies would cry when their mothers left the room, but would calm down after a few minutes. Then, when their mothers returned, the babies were happy to see them. Sad to see you go, happy to have you back. The researchers labeled this as healthy attachment.

But other children reacted very differently. When their mothers left, they would cry inconsolably or not react at all. When the mothers returned, these children seemed indifferent or resentful.[11] The latter group was classified as having unhealthy attachments to their caregivers.

Subsequent studies found that children with "anxious" or "avoidant" attachments faced a host of emotional and physical challenges. One of the harmful effects of unhealthy attachment: the children are unable to handle stress and regulate their emotions and behaviors.[12] Their ability to bond with their primary caregiver compromised their ability to control themselves.

The findings show us just how crucial it is for children to form healthy attachments to their parents (I think I'll go give my kids a hug right now). It also led to another intriguing line of inquiry. What if the same principles of attachment apply to our relationship with God?

Researchers tackled that very question. They found that people who have a secure attachment to God reap benefits similar to people who attach securely to their parents.[13] The inverse is also true: failure to form a healthy attachment to your heavenly Father creates many of the same problems as failing to attach to your earthly parents. Without a healthy attachment to God, we're more likely to fall prey to destructive thinking and behaviors. And some of those behaviors are very serious. Studies show that people with an "anxious attachment" to God are more likely to suffer from paranoia, neuroticism, and eating disorders like bulimia.[14]

People who have a secure attachment to God reap benefits similar to people who attach securely to their parents.

In one way it shouldn't be surprising to find this link. After all, the Bible's dominant title for God is "Father." We are His children. It makes sense that our ability (or inability) to form a secure attachment to our heavenly Father would carry serious implications. My friend Duane Sherman, a student of the spiritual disciplines, believes a healthy attachment to God is foundational to spiritual growth. He explained it to me like this:

> Many of the people who have engaged in spiritual disciplines for decades have not made the spiritual gains they would have hoped. Why is that? There's often something deeper going on. We all have addictions or hang-ups or coping mechanisms. Going back to heal the broken parts of us is key to soul formation. We need to form new habits and practice the disciplines, but that's step Number Two. First we have to go back and eliminate these coping mechanisms, these false sources of joy and love, through a secure attachment to God.

Developing that secure attachment will look differently for everyone. There are no formulas or quick fixes when it comes to this kind of deep soul work. But at the end of the day, attaching securely to God is about getting grace, not just as a theological concept, but a truth that penetrates our hearts. It means knowing at a core-deep level that we're forgiven, justified, and redeemed. It means resting in God's unconditional love and acceptance.

When this happens, our behavior changes. Grace allows us to mature. Like children with healthy attachments, we won't freak out any time we sense God's absence. Nor will we withdraw in cold indifference. It enables us to regulate our emotions and behavior, knowing we're secure in the arms of our loving Father. It helps us exercise self-control.

"DO THE HARD THING"

When the English cleric John Stott died in 2011, tributes came pouring in. Billy Graham lamented the loss of his friend, calling him "one of the evangelical world's greatest spokesmen."[15] Rowan Williams, the Archbishop of Canterbury, praised Stott for his "graciousness and deep personal kindness" and life "of unsparing service and witness."[16] Even *Time* magazine, which had named Stott as one of their 100 most influential people, ran a warm obituary calling him "one of the world's most influential and popular Evangelical figures."[17]

Despite living in the same London neighborhood for his entire life, Stott made a major impact on Christians around the world. He was the chief drafter of the Lausanne Covenant, a global manifesto calling the church back to evangelism. He also wrote more than fifty books and ran a ministry equipping Bible teachers in the Global South.

Stott was the quintessential English gentleman: learned, refined, and unerringly gracious. Yet beneath the decorum, was a man of unusual discipline. Arising at 5:00 a.m. every morning, the lifelong bachelor kept a grueling speaking and writing schedule. He was always quick to serve others. In the wake of his death, the Latin American theologian René Padilla remembered being struck by this attribute.

On the previous night we had arrived in Bariloche, Argentina, in the middle of heavy rain. The street was muddy and, as a result, by the time we got to the room that had been assigned to us, our shoes were covered with mud. In the morning, as I woke up, I heard the sound of a brush—John was busy, brushing my shoes. "John!," I exclaimed full of surprise, "What are you doing?"

"My dear René," he responded, "Jesus taught us to wash each other's feet. You do not need me to wash your feet, but I can brush your shoes."[18]

Another ministry leader recalled the time he brought Stott in to speak to a group of pastors. The elderly Englishman arrived late at night and met with his host to discuss the format for the next day. The man assured the legendary cleric that the men were expecting a casual affair. He urged Stott "to reflect on what he had already written." But that didn't sit well with Stott.

> When I told him this, he was quiet and looked away for about a minute—a long minute. He then said, "That will never do. These men have come long distances and having a free form discussion is a disservice to them. We'll have to have something for them to discuss."[19]

The man reassured Stott that preparing an original talk was unnecessary, but the next morning he found Stott at breakfast preparing his remarks. "He had stayed up most of the night preparing on topics he thought relevant to their ministries. When we convened the group, it was clear they were going to be treated to the fruits of his 'all-nighter.'"[20] Sure enough, the pastors drank in the words he had prepared specifically for them.

> No one complained. No one interrupted. No one left the room for a full four hours. They knew they were the fortunate recipients of a rare opportunity as John discoursed

on topic after topic and they scribbled notes. It was only at the break for lunch that they had a chance to ask questions—and they did!

John kept up that pace for three days, and when we concluded he was going strong while everyone else was dragging. I've never seen anything like it since.[21]

Stott's actions that day were a perfect example of his belief about the purpose of self-control. "Why do I say that love is balanced by self-control?" he once asked in a sermon. "Because love is self-giving, and self-giving and self-control are complementary, the one to the other. How can we give ourselves in love until we've learned to control ourselves? Our self has to be mastered before it can be offered in the service of others."[22]

That's what Stott did that night—and on countless other occasions. He exhibited self-control in service of others. In the final days of his life, he gave these last words to his longtime assistant: "Do the hard thing."[23] That's precisely what John Stott did over and over and over throughout his life. Not for himself, but for others. Not only in his power, but buoyed up and carried along by the power of the Holy Spirit.

Go and do likewise.

Self-Control Training:
Entry #7—Fasting Continued

MY LEGS ARE WEAK, HEAD SWIMMING. I teeter on the verge of fainting. In my delirium, I grope for something to support me, but find nothing. I see mirages—milkshakes, burgers, pizza—they flicker invitingly, only to vanish as I approach. Then I hear a voice.

"Oh, stop acting like a baby. You've only missed two meals."

The voice belongs to my wife, and she isn't impressed with how I've been moping around the house. She's right about my theatrics, but dieting—even for one day—is harder than I'd anticipated. Missing breakfast was fine. But by lunchtime, my stomach growled. By dinner I was dizzy. And sad.

I love the idea of fasting. That morning, I was feeling pretty spiritual. I read my Bible and spent some time in prayer. I was looking forward to the day. I'd use the time when I'd normally spend eating to commune with God. But then the hunger and weakness set in and my attitude soured. By 9:00 p.m. I was famished. Instead of praying, I sat on the couch staring blankly at the TV. That's when I heard the voice again. This time it was warm, compassionate. "You're miserable," my wife said. "We have leftovers from dinner. Why don't you just eat some chicken and mashed potatoes?"

This is how temptation comes, I thought through the fog of my hunger. Sweet, appealing. There was even an angel of light. I took her up on the offer. Fasting fail #3.

When I think about fasting, I'm conflicted—and not just because it's difficult to do. It goes deeper than that. I have mixed motivations. Am I fasting to lose weight and look better? Or am I doing it for spiritual reasons? There's nothing wrong with wanting to lose weight (and let's face it, I could afford to drop a few pounds), but I wonder if that motivation is ultimately strong enough. In chapter 2 we looked at what researchers call sanctified goals—objectives that serve some ultimate end. Study after study has found that people who have some overriding purpose for their goals are far more likely to accomplish them. Motivations matter. And I don't know if looking better in a mirror is motivating enough.

Recently I've been following a friend's weight-loss journey through her posts on Facebook. In her latest post, she announced that she'd lost a total of sixty-one pounds. In the new picture she posted of herself, she smiled broadly. She was almost unrecognizable from the photo she'd taken mere months before. But it wasn't the weight loss that impressed me most; it was her reasons for doing it.

> I press on even when the scale is not cooperating. I press on when I'd really rather eat something else. I press on when it is hard and I want to quit. I'm focused on my *whys*. I want to be able to take my girls on a roller coaster. I don't want to go on medications because I can't manage my weight and my diet. I want to live a long and healthy life for my girls and future grandchildren. And I want to feel good about myself and buy cute clothes again. I want those things more than I want a cheeseburger.

I guess you could say my friend had some superficial motivations. She longs for the day when she could "buy cute clothes again." But her main motivation is her children. She wants to be there for them—and that enabled her to press on even when things got tough. Her example inspired me, and helped me think more clearly about my motivations for fasting. It's probably okay to have some physical motivations, but the ultimate purpose of the practice should extend beyond myself.

A few days later I tried fasting again. The gnawing hunger, dizziness, and bad mood all came back with a vengeance. Yet this time, I pushed through. It was only one day, but I was starting to glimpse the spiritual benefits. No visions or mountaintop experiences. For me, the spiritual benefits were found in the opposite direction. When you fast, you're weak, vulnerable. You slow down. Your energy levels drop, and there's a sort of stillness to your life. You're empty—literally. It's an excellent reminder that you're finite, dependent. It might not feel great, but spiritually speaking, it's not a bad place to be.

Next, I decided to give the Daniel fast (the bagel-free version) a second try. For ten days, I'd eat nothing but fruits and vegetables. I'm not a fan of vegetables unless they're on pizza. Even then, I sometimes pick them off. So I decided I'd make fruit and veggie smoothies. I pulled the blender out of retirement and loaded up on produce. I used frozen veggies and fruit. It's amazing what you can eat if it's cold. My kids even got in on the act, squealing for "Daddy drinks" every time I took out the blender.

It was still tough. For a guy whose idea of health food is a bacon cheeseburger with light mayo, the diet was jarring. For the first four days, my head was in a fog. Fortunately, once my stomach got used to the new regimen, it got easier. Plus it was nice to see the numbers on the scale falling. At the end of the ten days, I was down ten pounds. And weight loss wasn't the only benefit. A few things I noticed during the fast . . .

I'm an automatic eater. During my fast, I was struck by how often I reached for food, just unconsciously. At one point, I popped a small cookie into my mouth and remembered I was fasting a nanosecond before biting down. I spit it into the garbage, bidding a reluctant farewell to the forbidden morsel. It reminded me of the research on habits. A lot of my poor eating decisions aren't even really decisions. They're habits. I'm on autopilot when I cram a lot of unhealthy food into my mouth. The fast slowed me down and made me aware of my eating choices. Hopefully I'll be more conscious of what I eat in the future.

Discipline has a price. Fasting involves two kinds of sacrifices. First, you give up the freedom to satisfy that most basic, human yearning—hunger. That's painful, but fasting has social consequences too. One young woman, Sophie DeMuth, reflected on this reality when she did the Whole30 diet. "For me, the 30-day challenge created unwanted distance between me and my friends and family," she wrote. "My limited diet clashed against their freedom to eat whatever they wanted."[24]

I can identify. You don't realize how much of your social life revolves around food until you stop eating. Even in the space of ten days, I felt it. We hosted a couple of dinners, which I sat through sipping water. I went out to restaurants with my wife and kids and had to abstain. Fasting can make you feel like an outsider, even when you're with family. But discipline always has a price. DeMuth went on to write, "Other acts of self-discipline come with their own set of losses: an earlier bedtime, shortened moments at home, or fewer places to hangout. Each sacrifice grinds against the norms of the world around us."[25] Fasting is no different. It comes with a cost.

Fasting is about gaining. From a biblical perspective, the goal of fasting isn't just self-denial. We Christians aren't grim ascetics who love to punish ours bodies. And it certainly isn't to prove how spiritual you are. Fasting, I've come to realize, is about replacing. It's giving up something physical to gain something spiritual. The Anglican bishop Todd Hunter puts it this way: "The stopping, the self-denial inherent in abstinence is meant to *start*, continue, and yield progress in the spiritual life. Its goal is to clear space and make room for something new."[26] When I fasted, it freed up time and attention to focus on God and examine myself. Saying no to physical hunger gave me an opportunity to seek spiritual nourishment.

I ended the ten-day period feeling physically and spiritually refreshed. I've decided to make fasting a regular part of my life. Maybe I'll fast once a month. Or a few times a year . . . let's not get crazy.

Chapter 8

Disciplined Living in an Age of Distraction

Strategies for Self Control in the Digital Era

"We are a people on the verge of amusing ourselves to death."

—NEIL POSTMAN

I'm writing these words from the Seventh Circle of Dante's *Inferno.*

Well, that's what I call it. My kids call it "Chuck E. Cheese's," and they think it is heaven. Right now, they're running around slapping buttons, whacking moles, spinning wheels, and shooting tiny basketballs into tiny hoops. I'm over here at the corner table eating cheap pizza and trying to write something intelligible. It isn't easy to do amid the flashing lights, blaring games, and shrieking children. (Oh, and did I mention there's a guy in a mouse costume running around high-fiving everyone?)

Pray for me in my hour of need.

As I sit here trying to concentrate, a thought occurs to me. The outside world is becoming more and more like this place. No, there aren't people running around in giant mouse costumes. I'm talking about the distractions, the noise. Life has gotten louder, chaotic, and more disruptive. And just like at Chuck E. Cheese's, a lot of the cacophony comes via screens.

There are the familiar diversions like TV, which, despite the advent of the internet, Americans continue to watch on average for more than five hours a day.[1] Advertisements bombard us from every angle, more than at any other time in history. In addition to these distractions, the internet has spawned a host of tools—like email, apps, social media, and online games—to grab even more of our time and attention. The average American now spends almost eleven hours a day staring at a screen.[2] Throw in eight hours of sleep (which we should be getting, but aren't), and that leaves a paltry six hours in which we risk making eye contact with another human being.

Self-control has always been hard. In every generation, Christians had to battle the flesh and the devil. But today the battle is different. It now involves resisting online porn and internet trolls. It requires not blowing money you don't have on apps and one-click purchases. It means not frittering away hours scrolling through your Facebook feed or crushing digital candies on your phone. I'm not saying new media is all bad. It can enrich our lives when used properly and in moderation. But we'd be fooling ourselves if we didn't recognize its drawbacks. If we're serious about developing self-control we need to be aware of how new technologies tax our restraint.

I wish I could lecture you on the dangers of new media from Mount Solitude, where I pass my days in silence and prayerful meditation. But alas, I live in the proverbial valley, immersed in the distracting technology that has become the hallmark of modern life. Recently I saw a report showing the average American house now has seven digitally connected devices.[3] I scoffed at the excess, then started counting the devices in my own home and came to a humbling realization: we have eight.

My online accounts have proliferated too. Every day I sign into three different email accounts and I check them compulsively. To modify a verse from the Bible, as a dog returns to his vomit, so I keep checking work-related email, even on weekends.

Of course email is just the tip of the digital iceberg. There's also social media. I'm on Facebook, Twitter, Instagram, Pinterest (hey, it's for guys too), Google Plus, and LinkedIn, even though I don't remember signing up for those last two. Most of these services are accessed through my smartphone, my ever-present help in times of boredom. It continually dings and buzzes and beeps, assuring me that I'm connected and popular and entertained. The other day I got stuck in line at Chipotle for twenty minutes and made a horrifying discovery: I didn't have my phone with me. I grew uneasy. My hand kept searching my pockets in vain for the glowing device. I was shocked by just how hard it was for me to stand there with nothing to do. I got so desperate I almost resorted to talking to the people around me!

I may be exaggerating a little, but every so often I get a glimpse of my digital dependency (usually when my devices are taken away), and it's not pretty. And I know I'm not alone. Americans check their phones on average 150 times a day and stare at them for approximately a quarter of their waking hours. I know that any discussion of self-control would be incomplete without addressing this issue.

The church father Justin Martyr named four major challenges to discipleship for the early Christians: sexual immorality, magic, wealth, and ethnic hatred.[4] Nearly two thousand years later, what has changed? I don't know about you, but magic isn't a major temptation for me. At least not the kind of magic that involves wearing pointy hats and casting spells. But author Andy Crouch noted that our technology makes a decent stand-in for the magic that was so alluring to our spiritual ancestors.[5] If you swap technology for magic, we pretty much have the same list today.

So how exactly do our magical technologies impact our self-control? The first way: by shoving every conceivable temptation in our face.

EXTREMELY LOUD AND INCREDIBLY CLOSE

The internet hasn't created any new temptations. It's just heightened the ones that were there all along. It's repackaged them, thrown a fancy new bow on top, and delivered them to your doorstep. It's made sin more accessible. For example, in the past, getting a hold of pornography was a risky, pride-swallowing enterprise. You had to walk into a store, approach the person behind the counter, and pay money for a dirty magazine—all while hoping that no one you knew witnessed the transaction. ("Well, hello Aunt Trudy. What are *you* doing here?")

The internet hasn't created any new temptations. It's just heightened the ones that were there all along.

Now thanks to the internet, sexual acts of every sickening variety are a click away—and available to view in the privacy of your home. I won't rehash all the staggering statistics about online porn, but one I saw recently hit me hard. Between 2015 and 2017, humans watched a total of one million years of porn—on just one website.[6] One million years! What a sad statistic. It would be impossible to quantify the minds warped, the marriages wrecked, by such habits. And on top of the destruction, what a colossal waste of time!

I recently heard the story of one courageous young woman who stood in front of her church to share her online struggle. She wasn't addicted to porn, but her digital activities had led her into sin. After a bad breakup, she downloaded apps and started to have inappropriate interactions with a number of different men. "When I was having a bad day, instead of turning to God to fulfill me, I went to a dating app. I knew there were going to be 50 messages on there from people telling me how great I am. I became addicted to the attention of strangers."

When she started dating a nice Christian man, she thought her problems were over. But even after they got married, she felt the pull of those dating apps. She was still using them to send photos and have inappropriate conversations. "My husband was telling me every day that he loved me, that I was beautiful, but I was addicted to the constant messages from others." Freedom only came once she confessed her problem and made the hard decision to delete all of her dating apps and social media accounts. "I can't even have a LinkedIn account," she said. "It's still a struggle for me," she confessed. "It's an everyday choice I have to make, to find my worth in God, to know and believe the promises God has given to me."

Initially, she assumed her challenge was unique. "Maybe I'm a freak," she said through tears. "What's wrong with me? How can I still being doing this? But then I started talking to other young married Christian women and found out that I'm far from alone."

This isn't the only kind of temptation the internet amplifies; it offers up a host of other allurements as well. Social media is a veritable minefield for the soul. A few years ago I interviewed a group of pastors about their social media habits. One of the pastors sat silently in the meeting. "How about you?" I finally asked him, searching for eye contact. "Are you on Twitter?"

"Well, I used to be," he said. "But I don't do that anymore . . ."

Turns out he'd become so addicted to Twitter, his friends staged an intervention of sorts. The microblogging platform was draining his time and feeding his ego, so he had to let go, cold turkey.

A writer friend of mine, Brandon Smith, also decided to board the cold turkey train. He had thousands of followers on Facebook and Twitter but didn't like how social media fed his desire for approval. "I've often lived day-to-day spending more time looking at 'likes' and 'retweets'" than looking my own family in their eyes," he confessed.[7]

He also noticed it was souring his view of others. "Social media feeds my propensity to be cynical and contrarian," he wrote. "Off social media, I'm generally joyful and accepting. On social media, I'm generally annoyed and dismissive."[8]

Quitting social media wasn't an easy decision for Smith. As a writer he realized deleting his accounts would deprive him of a valuable way to reach readers. But Smith concluded that, for him, the spiritual benefits were worth it. "I'm least like Christ when I'm using social media. And I've finally decided to take Jesus's caution seriously, and cut out my own social media eye rather than lust over the approval and acclaim of others (Mark 9:43ff)."[9]

These experiences may be the extreme, but they show how platforms like Facebook, Twitter, and Instagram have a way of appealing to our worst instincts. Somehow they fuel pride and insecurity at the same time. Even as we puff ourselves up by posting flattering pictures of ourselves and spotlighting our achievements (subtly of course), we feel a pang of envy as we see the latest accomplishment of a friend or colleague. *Why don't I have a house like that? How are her children so perfect? Why did he get that promotion? What am I doing wrong?*

Of course a lot of this discontentment and insecurity is based on a mirage. Sure, some people vacation in Tangier and eat sushi on mountaintops, but most of the time their lives aren't that glamorous. More often they're in the burbs eating microwaved chicken nuggets and watching reality TV. They're just choosing to spotlight those moments to make their lives look as desirable as possible to others. The problem, as one pastor puts it, is that "we're comparing our behind the scenes to everyone else's highlight reel."[10] And when we do that, we become miserable. Just think of all the sins that stem from unhealthy comparisons: envy, covetousness, greed, and worry. Nothing fuels the comparison game quite like social media.

Nothing fuels the comparison game quite like social media.

The internet creates a similar dynamic when it comes to generating conflict. The Bible warns us against having "anything to do with foolish and stupid arguments" (2 Tim. 2:23). That's often the first commandment you break when going online. There is a lot of solid, thoughtful exchanges out there—but they rarely get the clicks, the shares, the millions of views, the endless scrolls of comments. Powerful algorithms actually favor more divisive exchanges because they drive traffic. Therefore the content that "wins" online draws us in with gleeful promises that so-and-so gets "owned" at the three-minute mark. Or proclaims that one person "destroys" another. Note how it's never "makes a good point" or even "wins the argument." No, destroys! C. S. Lewis wrote the following words about hell, but I can't help think they make for a pretty accurate description for a lot of social media:

> We must picture hell as a state where everyone is perpetually concerned about his own dignity and advancement, where everyone has a grievance, and where everyone lives the deadly serious passions of envy, self-importance, and resentment.[11]

Equally ubiquitous are the online takedowns and diatribes with click-bait titles that guarantee to overwhelm our outrage threshold. "Your Jaw Will Hit The Ground!" We may laugh at these transparent ploys to get our attention. Yet too often we fall prey to the hyperpolarized, winner-takes-all, the other-side-is-Hitler attitude. We stop conversing and start fighting. Emboldened by the anonymity the internet affords, we end up saying things to strangers we would never utter face to face.

DISTRACTING OURSELVES TO DEATH

There's another danger lurking online and it has nothing to do with explicit sins like lust, envy, or trolling—yet it's also devastating to our self-control. It has to do with what constant diversions and entertainment does to us at a neurological level. It turns out living in a Chuck E. Cheese world seriously undermines our ability to concentrate and engage in more demanding intellectual endeavors.

Recently the bestselling Christian author Philip Yancey made a surprising confession: he can't read anymore. Well, at least he can't read like he used to. Before describing his "personal crisis," he shared how he used to read: three books per week with an entire evening dedicated to consuming classics from the likes of Shakespeare and Dostoevsky. But something changed. "I am reading many fewer books these days, and even fewer of the kinds of books that require hard work."[12]

What happened? In short, the internet.

> The internet and social media have trained my brain to read a paragraph or two, and then start looking around. When I read an online article from *The Atlantic* or *The New Yorker*, after a few paragraphs I glance over at the slide bar to judge the article's length. My mind strays, and I find myself clicking on the sidebars and the underlined links. Soon I'm over at CNN.com reading Donald Trump's latest tweets and details of the latest terrorist attack, or perhaps checking tomorrow's weather.[13]

I was well aware of this phenomenon before I read Yancey's confession. I'd read *The Shallows* by Nicholas Carr, a book that explores how the internet fractures our concentration and shrinks our attention spans. I'd also read a sobering study showing that distraction from constant email and text messages resulted in a ten point temporary drop in IQ, more than double the loss of IQ points someone experiences while high on marijuana.[14] But somehow reading about Yancey's experience was especially unnerving. I expect the internet to dumb down those darn Millennials and "Screenagers." But Yancey is sixty-something, and a brilliant, prolific author. If his mind has been taken out by the internet, what chance do the rest of us have?

I've experienced the internet's powers of distraction in my own life. Earlier I mentioned how challenging it is for me to write. Even when I'm able to carve out time in my busy schedule, the task itself can be excruciating. And the internet hasn't made that any easier. Even as I sit here tapping out words on my computer, I hear the siren song of the web. I know that I'm just a click away from checking my email or Twitter or watching NBA highlights or reading the news. Mindlessly surfing the web would be such a welcome reprieve from the arduous task of wrestling words into sentences.

ADDICTIVE BY DESIGN

Why is the internet so addictive and distracting?

Because it's designed to be.

In 2017, the founding president of Facebook, Sean Parker, came out with some candid words about the social media giant he helped create. Most people think of Facebook primarily as a vehicle for reconnecting with old friends and family members. Publicly, Facebook speaks in lofty terms about making the world a better place and fostering community. But Parker said that from the outset, the goal was different: "How do we consume as much of your time and conscious attention as possible?" According to Parker, "exploiting a vulnerability in human psychology" was the way to accomplish this feat.

We need to sort of give you a little dopamine hit every once in a while, because someone liked or commented on a photo or a post or whatever. And that's going to get you to contribute more content, and that's going to get you . . . more likes and comments. It's a social-validation feedback loop . . . exactly the kind of thing that a hacker like myself would come up with.[15]

I don't know about you, but I find this admission a little spooky. The reason we get addicted to these platforms is no accident. They are sophisticated tools designed to manipulate our minds. Parker referenced dopamine, which is often called the brain's "feel-good chemical." It's released when you exercise, make a discovery, or accomplish something . . . or when you do drugs or gamble. In a famous experiment, rats could push a level to receive a dopamine boost. The chemical was so powerful that the rats ignored sex and food to keep getting a dopamine boost. They would even walk across an electrified grid, receiving painful shocks with each step, in order to reach the lever.[16]

Turns out we're all a little ratlike when it comes to this powerful neurotransmitter. In one study, researchers used MRI scans to study the brains of teenagers as they used social media. When the teens saw that someone "liked" one of their posts or pictures, the reward circuitry of their brains would light up. Lauran Sherman, the study's lead author, reported "This is the same group of regions responding when we see pictures of a person we love or when we win money."[17] When the teens saw a large number of likes on photos of themselves, the reward areas of the brain were especially active, motivating them to post more often.

The researchers noted that brains of teens are especially

sensitive to rewards, but we are all subject to this dynamic. It explains why when we're feeling down, we'll often turn to social media. If someone "likes" or shares one of our posts or pictures, the reward area of our brains are stimulated. Of course, highs never last long, so like gamblers pulling the handle on a slot machine in search of the next payout, we keep hitting "refresh," hoping for another like or comment. Some platforms have been accused of intentionally withholding "likes" to get users to log in more often.[18] Social media platforms are dopamine delivery systems.

We call dopamine the brain's feel-good chemical, but that's not quite accurate. Dopamine doesn't deliver pleasure; it makes you anticipate pleasure. It produces a state of arousal and desire. Dopamine floods your brain when you spot that chocolate cake through the restaurant window or see a sexually alluring image. Dopamine directs your focus toward the desired object and urges you to pursue it. But that feeling of excitement isn't exactly pleasure. In fact, if you can't fulfill the desire, it makes you miserable.

Remember the poor rats that kept hitting the lever for more dopamine? Researchers assumed that the dopamine hit must have sent the rats to Cloud 9. After all, they preferred it to even sex and food. But when they conducted a similar experiment with humans, they discovered the truth. Like their rodent counterparts, the human subjects kept hitting the button to receive more dopamine, but to the surprise of researchers they didn't say it felt good. It was just addictive. And it made them miserable, even as they wanted more.[19] This is what psychologist Kelly McGonigal calls "the brain's big lie," that we "find it nearly impossible to distinguish the promise of reward from whatever pleasure or payoff we are seeking."[20]

Social media has capitalized on this deception. It doesn't leave you content and satiated. Often it leaves you feeling disconnected. After a couple of hours on social media, you don't feel happy or satisfied.

Another former Facebook executive stepped forward recently to spill the beans about Facebook's impact. He was even more condemnatory than Parker:

> "The short-term, dopamine-driven feedback loops that we have created are destroying how society works. . . . We curate our lives around this perceived sense of perfection, because we get rewarded in the short term—signals, hearts, likes, thumbs up—and we conflate that with value and we conflate it with truth. And instead, what it really is is fake, brittle popularity that's short-term and leaves you even more . . . vacant and empty before you did it."[21]

That description rings true with me. Even if you manage to achieve a "fake brittle popularity" on social media, it often leaves you feeling "vacant and empty." And it's designed to leave you that way—it's what ensures you'll come back for more.

I'm not saying companies like Facebook and Twitter are sinister organizations bent on ruining the world. They're just doing what companies do—trying to maximize value for their shareholders by delivering audiences to advertisers. But it's worth noting that their ability to accomplish these goals involves capturing as much of your time and attention as possible. Google has taken the quest for our attention to absurd new heights. Beginning in the early 2000s, they pioneered A/B testing that strained even the patience of their engineers. They would test as many as forty-one shades of blue on their homepage to see which color

Their sole purpose is to steal as much of your time as possible. You've been warned.

encouraged greater engagement with their site.[22]

These are the lengths tech companies are going to grab and keep your attention. And it's unprecedented. For the first time in history, there are geniuses armed with limitless funds, mountains of data, powerful algorithms, and a profound understanding of human psychology. Their sole purpose is to steal as much of your time as possible. You've been warned.

THE TOLL ON YOUR SOUL

This constant distraction takes a heavy toll on your spiritual life. The internet isn't just after your brain; it wants your soul too.

When we talk about sin, we usually focus on understanding temptation. And for good reason: knowing your vulnerabilities is vital. It enables you to guard against enticements to which you're uniquely vulnerable. An alcoholic shouldn't hang out in bars. The shopping addict should avoid malls—and Amazon.com.

But while it's wise to focus on temptation, we need to pay attention to our state of mind too. We know that there are certain things that decimate our willpower. Being tired, for instance, leaves us more vulnerable to temptation. Ditto for being hungry and stressed. The same is true for being distracted. It's like a pickpocket who works with an accomplice. While one is distracting you, the other robs you blind. You don't even know what hit you.

Have you ever wondered why so many stores blast loud music or provide other diversions? They want you to act on impulse. It's not in their best interest to provide a distraction-free environment where you can think clearly and resist temptation. Studies have demonstrated that even mild distractions, like trying to remember a phone number, leave people more likely to make unhealthy choices.

The internet is like every store on earth rolled into one. It offers up an endless flood of distraction that wears down your resolve. Bombarded by this continual flow, we become easy marks for temptation.

At the same time, it makes it harder to engage in spiritual practices. Scripture reading is often the first to go. You may not care about plowing through dense classics, but as a Christian, you should care about reading at least one classic. Well, sixty-six classics if you want to get technical about it—the library of holy books we call the Bible. In chapter 6, we saw how Bible reading is a keystone habit, a practice that pays dividends in multiple areas of life. Yet let's face it—reading the Bible is difficult. It's a big, daunting book. Yes, it's the inspired Word of God and filled with breathtaking beauty. But it was written in multiple genres over thousands of years by people from ancient cultures. It demands discipline to read and understand.

Contemporary Christians tend to live off "Scripture McNuggets" rather than "feasting on the whole Word of God."

I interviewed Glenn Paauw of the Institute for Bible Reading about the Bible reading habits of contemporary Christians. One of his biggest concerns is how contemporary Christians tend to live off "Scripture McNuggets" rather than "feasting on the whole Word of God." To correct this habit requires "big readings of Scripture," he says. "We need to increase the size of our Bible readings. Start reading the words around your cherry-picked passages. Then you're immediately confronted with context. . . . I'm a big fan of reading entire books of the Bible."

Unfortunately, for people with Twitter-sized attention spans, doing "big readings" of an ancient text is nearly impossible. The internet trains us to skim instead of read. It also encourages what cognitive scientists call "task switching," a practice of shifting your attention from one thing to another. The problem is that each time you shift your attention—a practice the internet encourages constantly—the brain has to reorient itself. The practice imposes "switching costs" that slow your brain down and diminish your ability to concentrate. Here's how Stanford communications professor Clifford Nass explained the impact of constant switching on the brains of the subjects he studied. "People who multitask all the time can't filter out irrelevancy. They can't manage a working memory. They're chronically distracted. . . . they're pretty much mental wrecks."

Even when these habitual multitaskers got offline, the negative effects of the switching persisted. Nass continued:

> The people we talk with continually said, look, when I really have to concentrate, I turn off everything and I am laser-focused. And unfortunately, they've developed habits of mind that make it impossible for them to be laser-focused. . . . They just can't keep on task.[23]

Our brains are addicted to the novelty served up by the internet. No wonder we struggle to quiet our minds and study God's Word. Hip-hop artist and pastor Trip Lee attests to this dynamic in his own life: "The more time I spend reading ten-second tweets and skimming random articles online, the more it affects my attention span, weakening the muscles I need to read Scripture for long distances."[24]

In his book *12 Ways Your Phone Is Changing You*, Tony Reinke connects our ability to engage Scripture with our willingness to tune out online distractions.

> To live an abundant life in this insatiable consumer society, we must plead in prayer for God-given power to turn our eyes away from the gigs of digital garbage endlessly offered in our phones and tune our ears to hear sublime echoes of an eternal enthrallment with the transcendent beauties we "see" in Scripture.[25]

FAREWELL, SOLITUDE AND COMMUNITY

Another casualty of the digital flood is solitude. Once you've conditioned your brain to require constant entertainment, quieting your soul to commune with God becomes nearly impossible.

I sense this in my own life. When I try to carve out time for meditation and prayer, I feel a strong urge to reach for my phone or log on to my computer. I try to spend time with God but squirm with restlessness the moment I'm deprived of external stimuli. Connecting deeply with God takes silence, solitude, and concentration. It might even mean we have to get bored. But as my friend Skye Jethani says, "Boredom is a prerequisite to spiritual growth." That statement may sound wrong. In America, being bored is among the worst things that can happen to you, but I think he's onto something. As unendurable as it may be for tech-addicts like me, boredom just might be the answer. It can serve as a spiritual reset, a blankness into which God can speak. Of course spiritual practices aren't boring. If we fully grasped what we're truly doing (communing with the God of the universe!) we wouldn't be bored. We'd be excited, energized. But for people whose imaginations have been blunted by a barrage of digital stimuli, slowing down will feel like boredom, at least at first.

The internet makes spending time alone and with God more difficult. It also threatens our time with each other, straining at the cords of Christian community.

A couple of years ago, I was out for dinner with my family when I noticed a group of young people at the table next to us bowing their heads. *That's refreshing*, I thought. *You don't see too many young people pausing to pray before meals anymore.* I glanced back a few minutes later and was surprised to see them still frozen in the same position. That's when it hit me. They weren't praying; they were on their phones. I marveled at the irony of the scene. They were together but disconnected—at least from each other.

A pastor friend who leads a thriving urban church of mostly twentysomethings told me about how big a challenge this kind of behavior is for his congregation. "This is our church's greatest obstacle to discipleship," he said, holding up a smartphone. The young, affluent couples attending his church gave lip service to the idea of community, but had trouble breaking away from their digital devices to truly engage with each other. At the time of our conversation, my friend was thinking of placing baskets in the foyer of the church and having everyone drop their smartphones in before entering the sanctuary. He knew the idea would be a tough sell for his hyperconnected parishioners, but he was determined to find a way to wrest digital devices out of the hands of his distracted congregants, if only temporarily. "I don't know if that's the solution," he said, "but we have to do something."

BE THE TORTOISE

The people I've known who have had major moral failings all had one thing in common: they were moving way too fast. Their failures were tragic, but not surprising. We're like cars— far more likely to crash when moving at a high rate of speed. Cramming our schedules depletes our willpower and leaves us physically exhausted. It's the perfect recipe for a moral failure. Slowing down and resting replenishes our willpower reserves.

Slowing down enables us to defeat temptation. Our desires are strong, but short-lived. Sometimes by simply waiting ten minutes or so, the desire will wane, enabling you to resist giving in. Adopting practices that force you to slow your pace also help. Spending a mere five minutes in meditation or prayer boosts a person's willpower for the remainder of the day. Other studies have demonstrated that getting sufficient sleep and relaxation are crucial for shoring up willpower reserves.

No wonder Scripture repeatedly gives us commands such as "wait on the Lord" or "be still and know that I am God." Our Creator knows that we need to slow down and rest. When it comes to self-control, the tortoise beats the hare every time.

WEAPONS FOR FIGHTING BACK

Like most parents, I struggle to get my kids' attention. My six-year-old boy is particularly difficult. He's in constant motion. Whether he's playing tag with his sister, smashing toy superheroes into each other, or pretending he's a lizard that can scale vertical surfaces, the boy is a blur. That's fine; I'm pretty sure that's what little boys are supposed to do. The only problem comes when I need to tell him something important. He'll acknowledge my words with a mindless, "Yeah, Dad" as he blazes by, but I know he didn't really hear me. That's when I have to chase him down, remove whatever toy is in his hands, put my hands on his shoulders and look him in the eyes. Finally I have his attention.

I wonder if God feels the same way about His children sometimes. We're so busy, so distracted. New technologies have filled our lives with toys that keep us constantly entertained. Perhaps truly communing with our heavenly Father involves letting Him pull our toys from our hands long enough to hear Him again.

But how exactly do we do that? In order to protect ourselves from self-control-destroying technology, we need to exercise self-control in the first place.

Draw Bright Lines

We all want to improve our behavior. But often we pursue this goal with vague aspirations, like "I'm going to try to eat better." Of course, objectives like this rarely work because they're so ambiguous. "Bright lines" are hard-and-fast rules that help you avoid unwanted behavior. The term came from the legal system to describe clearly defined courtroom rulings, but researchers found the idea helpful for controlling conduct.

This is how it works. A vague goal like trying to eat better requires you to constantly assess what you should eat and how much. However, if you have a bright-line rule such as "No eating sugar" or "No eating after 8:00 p.m.," you're far more likely to see your eating habits improve. These rules may sound difficult but they actually preserve your willpower. When you see a donut, you know it has sugar, so it's off-limits. You don't have to sit around wrestling with a decision. You don't even have to think about it.

The Bible is filled with these sorts of "bright-line" rules. What are the Ten Commandments after all, but a series of inviolable laws designed to steer us away from evil? Jesus moved these bright lines into the realm of the heart. He taught us to not even lust or hate, knowing that those dangerous feelings are not only sinful but lead to outward acts of sin as well.

We're wise to apply this thinking to our lives, and not just to avoid committing adultery and murder. Bright lines are especially crucial for breaking bad digital habits.

My pastor, C. J. Coffee, is a bit of a Luddite. He doesn't spend much time online, isn't on social media, and he has (gasp!) an old-fashioned flip phone. He doesn't opt for these restrictions because he has something against technology. He does it to avoid falling prey to pornography. Since becoming a Christian in his late teens, C. J. hasn't looked at porn—not once. You might think that's because he's some sort of superman, but he says it's just the opposite. "I consider myself fundamentally weak in this area," he confessed. "That's why I've taken extreme precautions to avoid temptation."[26] He encouraged other people in our church to take the same measures if they find themselves besieged by temptation. "If you're a guy who's getting tempted by images online, don't be proud," he once thundered from the pulpit. "Set up controls on your computer. Don't access the internet when you're alone. And if you have to, get yourself a flip phone!"[27]

Even if you're not falling to porn, bright lines are valuable for limiting the influence of technology. Make hard-and-fast rules like "No email after 6:00 p.m.," or "No internet on weekends," or

"No phones at the dinner table." These bright lines are like levees, strategically placed in your life to guard against the flood of digital distractions that threaten to overwhelm your soul.

Structure Your Time

I doubt any of us sits down to plan the week and thinks, *Hmm . . . I'm going to pencil in thirty-five hours for staring at my phone, thirty hours of TV, and seven hours of mindlessly surfing the web.* Sounds ridiculous, right? We'd never plan to spend our time like this. Yet that's what many of us do—week after week.

How do we bring sanity back to our schedules? By becoming intentional about the way we spend our time. Of course that doesn't mean we say no more phones, TV, or computers. For most of us, that isn't feasible. If I said no to email, I'd lose my job! But it does require applying wisdom to our online habits. One tool I've found helpful comes from my friend Brett McCracken. Playing off Maslow's famous Hierarchy of Needs, McCracken came up with the "Wisdom Pyramid"[28] to give internet-addicted Christians a way to think more fruitfully about the way they spend their time.

As you can see, McCracken puts social media and the internet at the pinnacle of his pyramid—not because those are the best uses of your time, but because they're the least important. He advises prioritizing Scripture-reading and spending time with your church family in order to keep your priorities balanced.

These are good guidelines. I've often referred back to it when I sense that I'm inverting the pyramid in the way I spend my time.

Yet I also need more practical tools to help me allot my time wisely. Ironically, many of these tools are technological.

For those struggling with online porn, there are a host of great tools. You can download software like Net Nanny that will block

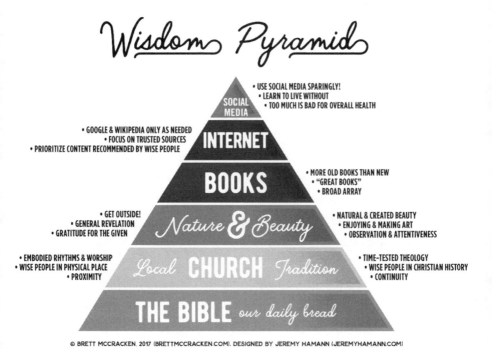

© BRETT MCCRACKEN. 2017 (BRETTMCCRACKEN.COM). DESIGNED BY JEREMY HAMANN (JEREMYHAMANN.COM)

all porn on your computer and phone. There are other services, like Covenant Eyes, that send a report of all your online activities to an accountability partner. You may feel a little silly installing software or paying for an accountability service, but it's worth it. Better to swallow your pride and spend a few bucks on a service, than risk polluting your mind and soul with the evils of online porn.

There are also small steps you can take to curb your digital dependency. One is to disable color on your smartphone. The former Design Ethicist at Google, Tristan Harris, explains that opting for the "grayscale" option makes the apps on your phone far less addictive.[29] A few months ago, I did something simple that reduced my tendency to waste time on my phone. I turned off all the notifications. Did I really need to be alerted every time someone liked one of my tweets or Facebook posts? Must I know each time CNN.com posts a new political story? Nope. Yet these dings and beeps were continually pulling me away from more important activities and sapping my ability to concentrate deeply. So I went into my settings and disabled all notifications. I haven't missed them. The second thing I did: install an app (called Moment) that tracks all the time I spend on my phone. It's sobering to get an accurate understanding of just how much time you're spending on your phone. Such tools help you prevent giving too much of your time and attention to the internet.

Make Your Sabbath Tech-Free

Observing a Sabbath is crucial. Don't worry—I'm not legalistic about it. The Jews observed the Sabbath on Saturday. The early Christians moved it to Sunday, the Lord's Day, to honor the day that Jesus rose from the dead. Today, we no longer live in tight-knit, kin-based cultures, and everyone has different work schedules. I don't care if you observe Sabbath on Sunday, Saturday—or Wednesday. But observing a Sabbath is wise, especially in our hurry-sick world.

A couple years ago, our family started giving our Sabbath a low-tech twist. We forbade the use of screens. We called it "No Screen Sundays." It's a little cheesy, but somehow the alliteration helped it stick. We don't always observe it in our home, but we try. And when we do, it feels like a little slice of heaven. The kids aren't zoned out watching cartoons, Mom isn't texting, and maybe most refreshing of all, Dad isn't glued to his phone checking email or Twitter. It's a day to worship God, enjoy our church community, and to be together as a family. Really together. "The

Sabbath prefers natural light to artificial light," writes A. J. Swoboda.[30] We've found this to be true in our home. When we power down our devices and step outside into the natural light of God's creation, our souls are restored.

This is just a sampling of strategies I've found useful. You may opt for different ones. The important thing is that we get intentional about freeing our minds from the tyranny of technology. Too much time in front of screens breeds impatience and impulsivity. It leaves us depressed and distracted and discontent. Compare those states of mind with the fruit of the Spirit: love, joy, peace, forbearance, kindness, goodness, faithfulness, gentleness, and—self-control. The contrast could hardly be sharper. By limiting our time online, we give God the space in our lives to cultivate the virtues He longs for us to have, including self-control.

Self-Control Training:
Entry #8—Running

SO FAR I'VE FOUND MY SELF-CONTROL EXPERIMENTS challenging. Yet, in one way, they've been easy. They don't require movement. Reading the Bible, praying, and fasting all demand discipline but you can do them all while sitting perfectly still on the couch. As a fairly sedentary person—and committed indoorsman—that's something I appreciate.

But that's about to change. The last discipline I'm going to try to build into my life is running.

At a recent checkup, I noticed my doctor was hinting at some lifestyle changes. And the hints weren't subtle. "Sometimes we eat even when we're not hungry," he said as he examined my shirtless torso. When he asked me if I exercised, I proudly reported that I try to get out for a walk a few times a week. "That's perfect . . ." he replied. I smiled—then he finished his sentence. ". . . if you were an eighty-five-year-old woman." Apparently he wasn't impressed with my afternoon strolls. "You need to get out there and do vigorous exercise," he told me. "You need to sweat."

That was another reason to start running—doctor's orders. I was excited. I was finally going to be *that* guy, the active, in-shape, tear-up-the-tarmac guy. But these romantic notions evaporated when I actually started running. Truthfully "running" is a generous term for what I was doing. It was more like plodding punctuated by stints of walking.

One of my favorite movies is *Chariots of Fire*. It's the classic film about the famous Christian Olympic runner Eric Liddell who refused to compete on Sundays. The movie opens with a famous scene of Liddell and his Olympic teammates running in slow motion on the beach. At one point Liddell explains his passion for running: "God made me fast. And when I run, I feel His pleasure."

I had Liddell's iconic words in mind when I went out for my first jog. But instead of flying over a track to the theme song from *Chariots of Fire*, I found myself shuffling around my block to the sound of my own wheezing. The only similarity to the movie: I too was moving in slow motion. When I came home, I complained to my wife: "God made me slow. And when I run, I feel His displeasure."

I went for my runs in the evening, right after work. But after about a week, they dropped in frequency. I was mentally exhausted from the day. Plus I felt a little guilty about leaving my wife with the kids for another half hour when she'd already been watching them all day. It was just the excuse I didn't need. Pretty soon I wasn't running at all. If I'm ever going to get in shape, I may need to try something else.

Chapter 9

Learning from Addicts

What Rehab Programs Reveal about Self-Control

"The devil always gives you the best stuff up front."

—BILL RUSSELL

I'm sitting in Bijou Café in downtown Portland with Bill Russell, the executive director of the Union Gospel Mission, a ministry that feeds the homeless and helps addicts turn their lives around. He utters the words above at the end of a monologue about the ravages of addiction.

"The best high you'll ever get is your first one, when the dopamine receptors in your brain are fresh," Russell tells me. "From there, it's all downhill. You take more and more drugs chasing that first high."

Once you're hooked, the game changes, he explains. Suddenly, it's not just about getting high. It's about avoiding pain. Stop using and you get "dope sick," street slang for the powerful withdrawal symptoms addicts experience when they stop using drugs. Being dope sick feels like getting the flu, but worse. "You get achy bones, zero energy, intestines are all roughed up, you're throwing up out of both ends," is how one opioid addict described it.[1]

And those are just the physical symptoms. According to DetoxTo Rehab.com, "The psychological effects of experiencing dope sickness may be so intense the person may consider suicide."[2]

Somehow, I'd never considered this side of addiction. I've always seen addicts as hopeless pleasure-chasers, but it would be more accurate to see them as pain-escapers. They're often driven to drugs to numb emotional or physical pain—and they keep going to avoid getting sick. That desperation leads to reckless behavior. "Once your money is gone, you'll break into houses, cars, anything to keep from getting sick," Russell says. Meanwhile, the drugs are damaging your brain, eroding your ability to make rational decisions. "That's why they'll shoot someone over $20 and not even bother to cover their tracks."

THE STAKES

As Russell described the grim reality of addiction, I felt a little guilty about the purpose of our conversation. After all, I wasn't there to help addicts; I wanted to know how addicts could help me. I had a hunch their journeys could teach me something about the nature of self-control. By definition, addiction involves an "inability to consistently abstain" due to "impairment in behavioral control."[3] Addicts are people whose self-control has been obliterated—and getting it back is vital. For some of us, self-control is about being more productive or losing an annoying habit. But for addicts, the stakes couldn't be higher. Self-control is a matter of life and death.

Six months prior to our conversation, Russell brought four men from the mission to our church to lead worship. They were part of a recovery program called LifeChange. They were talented musicians and spoke passionately about their love for Jesus. But when I showed up for my lunch with Russell I learned there was news about Jeremy, the quiet young man who played bass guitar for the group. One day Jeremy had gone for his daily jog and failed to return. He had spotted an orange syringe cap beside a curb; the kind heroin addicts discard after shooting up. What most people wouldn't have even noticed was a powerful trigger for Jeremy, and he relapsed. A few days later he overdosed and died.

I had met Jeremy only briefly. My wife and I shook his hand after the service, and thanked him for leading worship. Now I couldn't stop thinking about him. I remembered him in front of our congregation, playing guitar. I pictured him out for that fateful jog, filled with hope for the future. I thought of the growing number of addicts on the streets of Portland. Their journeys had started with a moment of chemically induced euphoria but had left them cold and sick and enslaved. Russell was right. The devil gives his best stuff up front.

Yet there's hope. Addictions can be conquered. Addicts can turn their lives around. For every tragic story like Jeremy's there's another of healing and freedom. I was curious. How do those recoveries happen? What does it take to wrestle the demons of dependency into submission? How can you build self-control from the ground up? And what can the rest of us learn from those who do?

ADDICTS 'R' US

The first lesson I've learned—and it's an uncomfortable one—is that I have more in common with addicts than I'd care to admit.

When I was twelve, my father planted an inner-city church with a soup kitchen. Because of this ministry to the homeless, it wasn't uncommon for people to show up at our church high or reeking of booze. We were often treated to slurred testimonies from addicts in the thick of the battle. "Jush a little under the weather tonight folks, but God is sho good."

One time my dad was preaching and made the mistake of posing a rhetorical question, "What would Jesus say to us today?" In the silence that followed, one of the soup kitchen regulars decided to hazard a guess. "I dunno," he blurted out. "Probably tell me to quit drinking and get a job!"

As a teenager, I regarded these addicts with a mixture of pity and, if I'm honest, amusement. Even as an adult I consigned their struggles to a category far removed from "normal," respectable people like me. It never occurred to me that I might have something in common with them.

In recent years, that illusion has crumbled. In this book, I've written about my brothers quite a bit. In the introduction, you met Darren. He's the one whose heart attack forced me to think seriously about my physical health and whose penetrating question alerted me to my lack of spiritual growth. In chapter 4 you met Dan. He was the perfect one, the spiritual prodigy whose early demonstrations of self-control made me wonder if there was hope for me. You may have wondered, *How many brothers does this guy have?* One more, as it turns out—my oldest brother, Dave.

As I've written this book, I've gone back and forth on whether to include Dave's story. It's not an easy one. In fact, it has rocked our family to its core. Dave is an addict. Even writing those words feels strange to me. At thirty years old, Dave's life was enviable. He was a financial consultant who earned a multiple six-figure salary. He was married with two kids. Everything seemed to be going great. But secret addictions were chipping away at the edifice of his life. Eventually it all came crashing down, costing Dave his marriage and career. He became estranged from his kids. He did a yearlong stint in rehab—then relapsed.

About a year ago, Dave's ex-wife was driving when she spotted a man in a hospital gown sitting at a bus stop. She looked closer and realized it was Dave. He'd overdosed and almost died, he told her, but had no memory of how he'd landed at the bus stop. After this brush with death, Dave vowed to change, but his resolution didn't last long. He continued doing drugs and started stealing cars to support his habit. Recently Dave was arrested after leading police on a high-speed chase in a stolen car. He is currently serving a four-year prison sentence.

I'm saddened each time I think about Dave's dramatic descent. How did he wind up in such a sad state? We pleaded with him to change, directed him to rehab, and staged an intervention. But was there more we could have done to help him? Will landing in jail finally give him the wakeup call he needs?

Dave's plight also causes me to look inward. What if I'm not so different from my brother? I used to think of addicts as "out there"—the beer-soaked guy on the side of the road begging for change or the sweaty stockbroker snorting cocaine off his desk. But now that addiction has hit close to home, I see things differently. The same destructive impulses that destroyed Dave's life are present in me. The difference between us is a matter of degrees, not kind. The science writer, David DiSalvo, looks at addiction from a neurological level and concludes, "What's alarming is that anyone's brain can theoretically become addicted to a substance or behavior, given enough exposure. And once that happens, the addiction pathways are open to accommodate additional compulsive behaviors."[4] Addicts are not an isolated subset of the

We have more in common with addicts than we might think. And it means we need to take the same steps addicts in recovery take if we hope to get free.

population. We all have the potential for addiction.

Even if we never engage in the activities that land us in jail, the Bible tells us that all sin has an addictive quality. "Everyone who sins is a slave to sin," Jesus said (John 8:34). That means we have more in common with addicts than we might think. And it means we need to take the same steps addicts in recovery take if we hope to get free.

NO SMALL SINS

Dave's problems seemed to come out of the blue, but in truth there were worrying behaviors that stretched back to childhood. He had a habit of borrowing people's possessions and failing to return them. (I can't tell you how many bikes he lost.) When he was thirteen years old, he took a summer job in a convenience store where he was exposed to pornography, and created a habit that plagued him as an adult. Dave wasn't outwardly rebellious. He was compliant and easygoing. When my parents assigned my brothers and me household chores, we'd drag our feet and argue. Dave, on the other hand, would happily comply with their commands—but never actually obey. He had a way of sidestepping responsibilities with little concern for the inevitable consequences.

None of these behaviors seemed too alarming. After all, it's not uncommon for teenagers to dodge responsibilities or peek at dirty magazines. Yet for Dave, these actions became the first stop on a long road that would end in destruction. The little sins went unchecked until they grew into more serious habits. As I watched my brother's life become a waking nightmare I couldn't help think of these words, written nearly two thousand years ago: "After desire has conceived, it gives birth to sin; and sin, when it is full-grown, gives birth to death" (James 1:15). The nun Elizabeth Scalia puts it this way: "The habit of sin is what is formed by permitting these 'little sins,' and the reason they 'mean a lot' is because once they become ingrained within us, they shape who we are: mentally, spiritually, and even physically."[5]

James described sin as a progression. At first, giving into temptation seems harmless. It doesn't even seem to impact your life. The problem is that sin doesn't stop there. Sin doesn't start big and scary. It's like a lion cub; at first it's cute and cuddly. But keep it around and feed it and one day it will overpower you. Sin grows, and when it is "full-grown" it destroys everything and everyone around you.

I imagine that if you dig into the history of most addicts, you'd find a similar story. They didn't wake up one morning and decide to be addicted to drugs or alcohol. Instead they fed certain vices and behaviors until they lost control. I realize that addiction is a complex issue, involving genetic and environmental causes. Yet sin plays a role too. I know it did with my brother.

Little sins went unchecked until they grew into more serious habits. The secret to self-control (as if there's just one) is to control yourself while you still can.

Addicts show us the hard bottom of sin's slippery slope. In the beginning, sin seems like no big deal, a naughty habit or innocent indulgence perhaps. But that's never where it stops. The secret to self-control (as if there's just one) is to control yourself while you still can. "Be killing sin or it will be killing you," theologian John Owen wrote. To keep sin from devouring you, kill it early.

ADMITTING DEFEAT

Alcoholics Anonymous (AA), the popular international recovery program, has helped millions of people get sober. Initially limited to helping alcoholics, the program's famous 12 Steps have been used to help people find freedom from a wide range of addictive behaviors, including drugs, gambling, and eating disorders.

To a lot of psychologists, the program's success is a bit of a mystery. Bill Wilson, a drunken stock speculator with no training in science or psychology, started AA in the 1930s. Over the years, the steps haven't changed to incorporate new findings about the biological and genetic roots of addiction. And yet it works. What's the secret? One clue can be found in the program's very first step: "We admitted we were powerless over alcohol—that our lives had become unmanageable."[6]

It's a strange starting point, isn't it? To declare you are "powerless" and that your life is "unmanageable"? Wouldn't articulating such helplessness just fuel poor behavior?

If the 12 Steps were written today, I doubt they would start with such a grim confession. Given our love affair with self-esteem and empowerment, we'd likely opt for some inspiring affirmation of our inner strength. "We admitted we had power over alcohol—and we have everything we needed to manage our lives." That would be a more positive and pleasant starting point. But it wouldn't be as effective. Bill Wilson wrote, "The principle that we shall find no enduring strength until we first admit complete defeat is the main taproot from which our whole Society (AA) has sprung and flowered."[7] Or as another recovering addict wrote, "Rock bottom became the solid foundation on which I rebuilt my life."

A willingness to admit defeat permeates the entire program. From depending on a higher power to conducting a "fearless moral inventory" of your life to "humbly" seeking the forgiveness, to "making amends," weakness is everywhere. Even the famous AA introduction, uttered in countless gymnasiums and church basements around the world, involves confessing your flaws. "Hi, my name is _____, and I'm an alcoholic."

In other words, this is who I am: weak, broken, in need of help.

It's no coincidence that AA has its roots in the Christian faith. Wilson's journey toward sobriety was initiated by a dramatic encounter with God, and he patterned the entire program on biblical precepts (he chose the 12 Steps because there were twelve apostles). The insistence on confessing our flaws and feebleness is thoroughly biblical. Repeatedly, Scripture commends confessing our sins to God and each other and even boasting in our weakness (2 Cor. 11:30). When we do, we make the same startling realization millions of addicts have discovered. Instead of being overcome by temptation, we find our behavior improving as we become wary of our sinful tendencies and open to divine strengthening. Paradoxically, admitting your lack of self-control is the first step to improving it.

START WITH STRUCTURE

At the Union Gospel Mission in Portland, the LifeChange program Bill Russell runs is highly structured. Participants wake up early (4:30 a.m. for one group, 5:30 a.m. for the other), then shower, dress, and eat. At 7:00 a.m. they have study hall and leadership training. Self-evaluations and chapel follow at 8:00 a.m. Then the workday starts. That's right. Forget the Hollywood rehab cliché about addicts lounging in a luxury spa. Participants of LifeChange work a full day at the mission, 9–5.

The schedule is rigorous by design. It teaches participants structure, routine. And it virtually eliminates any possibility of relapse. Initially they're not even permitted to go outside the building on their own. Although the schedule is demanding, it doesn't take a lot of self-control. Program participants don't have to motivate themselves; they just obey. This too is by design. Russell explains that the energy they would normally spend navigating the complex tasks of adult life (earning money, securing housing, buying and cooking food) can be directed to Bible study, recovery groups, assigned labor, mental-health counseling, and group activities. This allows each resident to settle into a low-pressure, low-anxiety life. All of their energy, Bill says, is directed toward spiritual formation and developing self-control.

After a few months in the system, the residents feel good about themselves. They're clean, deepening their spiritual lives, and sticking to a new schedule. The program doesn't last forever, of course. And that's when the real test comes. Russell says that one of the problems is participants tend to "confuse system-control and self-control." Some mistake success in the program for victory over their vices. But the program is an artificial environment. Eventually they'll have to return to the real world, with all the old stresses and temptations. For them to stay clean on the outside, Russell says, "external system-control needs to give way to internal self-control."

Still, the time spent in a regulated, stress-free environment is an indispensable step toward recovery. When system-control is in place, personal routines emerge and replace the chaos of addiction. Residents get the experience of being part of a team and doing productive work. "They begin to think clearly and assemble a new fresh worldview," Bill says.

What can the rest of us learn from a program like LifeChange? One lesson that jumps out at me is that conquering addictive behaviors requires drastic measures. No, we can't all check into a recovery program for a year. But sometimes getting the upper hand on a besetting sin requires eliminating temptation entirely for a period. By doing so, we clear our heads and allow new patterns of behaviors to emerge.

Let's say you're addicted to online pornography. It may be that the best way to purge the addiction from your life isn't just through prayer and accountability, as valuable as those things are. You might need to cancel your internet service for a year. It may be painful, but during that time you will taste freedom from the addiction, deepen your spiritual life, and form new habits. When you do hook up the internet (hopefully with some new precautions), you'll have a track record of purity and new patterns in your life that help you resist the temptation.

Or say your spending is out of control. You may want to check into spending rehab—not literally, but mentally. Commit to a period of time when you're not allowed to go near a mall, retail store, or shopping website. Once you've broken the addiction, you can reflect on why you've been relying on a shopping habit for excitement and find healthy replacement activities. Then slowly introduce shopping with some wise restrictions.

In our conversation, Russell compared addiction to a broken

Sometimes we need extreme restrictions to loosen the stronghold of sin. In the end, we find that confinement brings freedom.

bone. "When you break your leg, you need a cast," he said. "It's like that with addiction. Eventually, you have to start moving the leg again. But at the beginning, you need that rigid structure." I think that's true for addicts of all kinds. Sometimes we need extreme restrictions to loosen the stronghold of sin. In the end, we find that confinement brings freedom.

POWER OF COMMUNITY

To improve our self-control, we need God—and each other. When you look at how addicts recover, one truth stands out perhaps clearer than any other: they need community. This is something Russell stresses. "When participants transition out of the program, the most important choices they have involve *who* they spend time with, and *where* they feel like they belong."

Recently as I was waiting for a flight at the airport, a sixty-something man sat down next to me and whipped out a book. The title grabbed my attention: *I'll Quit Tomorrow: A Practical Guide to Alcoholism Treatment*. I asked him about it, and immediately regretted doing so. He was clearly embarrassed by the question. He shifted in his seat and flipped the book over to hide the title. "I'm writing a book on self-control," I told him. "That's why your book caught my eye."

These words seemed to ease his apprehension. "I've been clean for years, but I'm starting to help other people who have the same issue," he told me. What did he think about self-control?

"It's important," he said. "But if you just rely on self-control, you're dead. You need a community around you. I know alcoholics who haven't had a drop for forty years and still go to the AA meetings."

I marveled at the idea of someone clean forty years, still dutifully driving to meetings, pulling up a metal chair in some dingy gymnasium, and introducing himself as an alcoholic. Why would he do that? "There's no such thing as an ex-alcoholic," the man at the airport said, suddenly very serious. "They know they still need the support." For addicts, community isn't optional. Like my new friend said, without it you're dead. Even those who stay sober for decades need it.

Support groups such as Alcoholics Anonymous demonstrate the importance of a social network to bolster self-control. We tend to think of self-control as a solitary virtue; it's just me squaring off against temptation. But the people we spend time with dramatically affect our ability to regulate our behavior. Hundreds of studies have demonstrated the powerful effects peers have on our behavior. We're actually wired for this influence. Our brains are equipped with "mirror neurons," that help us discern what people around us are thinking and feeling. These specialized neurons enable us to empathize with others and even "feel" their pains and desires. Of course when it comes to behavior, this unique ability cuts both ways. Willpower failures are contagious, but so is virtue. Psychologist Kelly McGonigal writes, "You can catch self-control as well as self-indulgence."[8] There's a reason your parents didn't want you hanging out with those "bad influences" in high school. They were right to be concerned.

Scripture warns, "Bad company corrupts good character" (1 Cor. 15:33). It also speaks of the benefits that come with hanging around the right kind of people: "As iron sharpens iron, so one person sharpens another" (Prov. 27:17).

By spending time with people who encourage us and hold us accountable, we give ourselves the best chance at improving our behavior. One crucial way to do this is by cultivating one of the keystone habits we discussed in chapter 6: church attendance. Meeting regularly with like-minded believers reinforces righteous behavior. Part of the reason Paul urged the early Christians not to neglect gathering together was because it was an opportunity "to stimulate one another to love and good deeds" (Heb. 10:24 NASB).

If you have an ongoing struggle with a specific sin, it's wise to seek out a group of fellow strugglers. Yet picking the right group of friends to keep you accountable is key. Research has shown there's a happy medium when it comes to finding the right support network. Joining a group of chronic failures will drag you down. Hanging around only with super saints can have the same effect. The key is to align with a group of people with similar goals and similar struggles.[9] Part of the reason AA is so effective is because it surrounds recovering alcoholics with recovering alcoholics. If an alcoholic seeks out people who have never touched a drink, they wouldn't benefit as much. On the other hand, hanging out with old drinking buddies guarantees a relapse. What they need are fellow strugglers, people who can come alongside them with both empathy and encouragement.

The worst thing you can do is battle temptation alone. When it comes to self-control, lone rangers are dead rangers.

The worst thing you can do is battle temptation alone. When it comes to self-control, lone rangers are dead rangers. To control ourselves, we need others.

DIVINE DEPENDENCE

Another aspect of AA that puzzles secular psychologists: the central place it gives to God. Even though AA opts for generic language like "Power greater than ourselves" and "God as we understood Him," seeking divine assistance is integral to the program. Six of the twelve steps mention God and one speaks of a "spiritual awakening." After confessing their own weakness in Step 1, alcoholics "believe that a Power greater than ourselves could restore us to sanity" and then "turn our will and our lives over to the care of God."[10]

In *The Power of Habit*, Charles Duhigg examines AA at length, describing it as "the largest, most well-known and successful habit-changing organization in the world."[11] He writes that part of AA's success comes from how it enables participants to replace bad habits with good ones. "AA succeeds because it helps alcoholics use the same cues, and get the same reward, but it shifts the routine," he writes.[12] Duhigg observes that AA's "system of meetings and companionship" provides the perfect replacement for the activity of drinking. When tempted to drink, AA members can turn to a warm community of recovering alcoholics rather than going on a bender at the bar.[13]

But Duhigg admits that habits don't explain all of AA's success. He cites research showing that habit replacement works for alcoholics—but only up to a point. If they have a major stressful event in their life, like the loss of a loved one or serious health problem, they often relapsed. Yet, as Duhigg reports, "those alcoholics who believed . . . that some higher power had entered their lives were more likely to make it through the stressful periods with their sobriety intact." The power of belief shocked and frustrated researchers. "Researchers hated that explanation," Duhigg writes. "God and spirituality are not testable hypotheses."[14]

Such findings shouldn't surprise Christians, however. We know the wisdom of surrendering to God. It's how we access the power to live a holy life. Apart from Christ, we can do nothing (John 15:5). Surrender is also essential for *not* doing things that we shouldn't. After all, the Bible's prescription for resisting the devil is not to declare your strength and self-sufficiency. It's to first submit yourself to God (see James 4:7).

Why does this surrender enable self-control?

Duhigg dismisses the idea of divine intervention. "It wasn't God that mattered," he writes. "It was belief itself that made a difference." From a secular perspective, I'm sure that explanation is partly true. In chapter 2, we saw the power of "sanctified goals." When we attach ultimate significance to our pursuits, we dramatically increase the likelihood of success. It's not necessary to invoke the supernatural to explain this; it's just a psychological principle. Infusing an activity with ultimate significance strengthens our ability to do it. And there's nothing more ultimate than God.

Yet as a believer I know there's more than psychology at play. The Bible is filled with promises of divine sustenance and strengthening for those who surrender to God. It's not like we're puppets, controlled without effort. We don't "let go and let God." Like we saw in chapter 7, our effort should not be pitted against divine empowerment. Rather, as we give control to God, He empowers us to be able to flee sin and pursue righteousness. As Erwin Lutzer writes, "You become stronger only when you become weaker. When you surrender your will to God, you discover the resources to do what God requires."[15] Surrender becomes the engine of self-control.

THE MORE SATISFYING WAY

During my conversation with Russell, I felt like all the research I'd done on self-control was coming together. I kicked off this book with the observation that a loss of self-control always results in a loss of freedom. Addicts serve as dramatic reminders of this principle. Many lose their freedom literally, like my brother locked up in prison. Even those who manage to dodge the authorities live under the tyranny of their chemical dependency.

In chapter 3, I argued that it's essential to understand our sinful nature and limited willpower. For some of us, that's difficult to accept. We prefer to see ourselves as strong and essentially good. Addicts, on the other hand, have learned the reality of sin the hard way. The ones who've been through recovery know that admitting their weakness is a crucial first step toward finding freedom.

The recovery process also highlights the importance of habits. Russell walks participants of LifeChange through the habit loop, teaching them how to recognize cues and change their routines. "The Holy Spirit gives self-control when we alter our old unproductive and less satisfying routines into new productive and more satisfying routines," Russell told me. He also addressed the paradox at the heart of this book—that it in the end, self-control isn't reliant on the self. "It's not a self-help thing," Russell said. "It is a fruit of the Spirit, so it's not merely us controlling ourselves."

Having an ultimate purpose is integral to recovery as well. Virtually every addict on the road to recovery cites a bigger purpose for getting clean. It might be a child or spouse or their faith in God. The key is to identify something bigger than themselves that can inspire them to keep their resolution firm when in the valley of temptation. For Russell and the participants in LifeChange, God isn't an optional add-on. God is central to the program's success. "Ultimately it comes down to a decision," Russell said. "Are you going to believe that the way of Jesus is more satisfying than the old way?"

That's a good question for all of us, addict or not. Are you going to believe that the way of Jesus is more satisfying than the old way? If you believe it—*really* believe it—you will start walking in that new way. You will resist temptation and cultivate holy habits. You will put your flesh to death by the power of God's Spirit. You will fight the good fight. You will stay rooted in divine reality so the fruit of self-control can grow in your life.

As you do, you'll find new levels of joy and flourishing. Your life won't be easy (in fact, at first it might be harder), but it will be deeper and more dynamic. It will be purposeful and productive. It will be holy, a life that blesses others and glorifies your Creator.

Of course, Satan comes alongside you to whisper his lies. "Jesus' way won't really satisfy you," he hisses. He trots out his shortcuts and promises instant pleasure and unlimited power. But by now you recognize the deception. You've seen it all before. You know he always gives you the best stuff up front—and makes you pay everything down the road.

God, on the other hand, is more interested in your future self. He's more concerned about you than your current level of comfort. He cares more about who you're becoming than how you feel right now.

And while the devil gives his best up front, God always saves the best for last.

Self-Control Training:
Entry #9—Full Court Press

About a month passed without a run. I'd basically given up. Maybe running was the problem. I needed an exercise I enjoyed more. I've read plenty of experts say that the best way to get in shape is to find an activity you really love. Hiking, rollerblading, kite surfing, whiffle ball, underwater hockey—the specific sport isn't important, as long as you enjoy it. If you enjoy doing it, the thinking goes, you'll keep doing it. The best exercise regimen is the one you stick with.

I like basketball, and I wasn't bad at it. I played in high school and for one year of college. Of course, that was twenty years—and fifty pounds—ago. It had been eons since I played a game of full-court basketball. Thankfully our church had a weekly basketball night. My wife had been pestering me to go, but I always found some excuse. "I need to get in shape before I go do that," I told her. It had never occurred to me that going out and playing with the guys might actually be the way to get in shape.

So I decided to show up. I felt like I was going off to war. My hands trembled as I laced up my old high-tops. I knew the other guys who played weren't exactly LeBron James, but they played regularly and I was completely out of shape. After warming up for a few minutes, we divided into teams and the game was on. I was shocked to see my first few shots go in, though I tried to mask my surprise.

Then the second game started. A player on the opposing team pointed a finger in my direction and said something I chose to take as a compliment. "Guard the old guy, he can shoot." Yes, I could shoot, but it turns out I couldn't run. In that second game, my lungs started to burn, and my legs turned to rubber. Suddenly the twentysomething I was guarding was galloping past me for easy layups. I briefly considered faking an injury, but figured lying to fellow church members probably qualified as a sin, and a weird sin at that.

When the game was over (which we lost), I informed the guys I had to go. But they wouldn't have it. "C'mon, stay for one more game," they said. One game turned into two and at the end of the night, I limped off the court exhausted. I was sore for a week.

But the next Monday night, I was back. This time I arrived too late to warm up, which turned out to be a mistake. On the second play of the game, I drove into the key, did a perfect crossover, and felt a stabbing pain in my back. I crumpled to the floor like I'd taken a bullet. It turns out I'd pulled a muscle between my ribs. Injuries are nothing to be ashamed of, though there's something slightly embarrassing about sustaining one when no one even touched you.

That rib took a few weeks to heal, and by the time it did, I was a little gun-shy about going back. Plus, the basketball games were held only once a week, and it was a good half-hour drive for me to get there. I still wanted to play basketball, but I decided if I really wanted to get in shape, I'd have to get back to running.

I started plodding around my block again, but this time I stumbled upon a routine that helped enforce my running regimen. Every day at 4:00 p.m. my son is dropped off at the bus stop a few blocks from our house. Since he's in kindergarten, someone has to be there to pick him up. Usually my wife does it, but one day I volunteered. "I'll just do my run and then pick him up," I said. "I can work for an extra thirty minutes after."

That turned out to be the perfect "cue" to go for a run. Every day I know that I must be at that bus stop at 4:00 p.m. I might as well do my thirty-minute run at the same time. In fact, it turned out to be the perfect habit loop. There was a "cue" (having to go pick up my son), a routine (the run), and a reward (at the end I got to see my son!). To date I've logged sixty-eight runs.

That doesn't mean it's easy. The first two weeks were awful. But I'm learning to fight through discomfort. Establishing good habits always feels difficult, even unnatural, at first. Breaking the inertia of your old ways of life takes effort and grit. But it gets easier as you go. After a while, I was surprised to find I was even looking forward to my run. I started to crave the "endorphin high" runners talk about. And I was losing weight and feeling more energetic. As with any new discipline, it starts with difficulty but ultimately leads to freedom.

Conclusion

Life under Control

My Prayer for You

Self-control isn't the sexiest topic."

I must have repeated that line to dozens of people during the course of writing this book. I'm not sure why I felt the need to hedge on the subject. Maybe I worried it didn't have enough excitement or sizzle.

"What's your book about?"

"Self-control. I know, I know. Not the sexiest topic."

In one way, I was right. After all, people don't write songs about self-control. It doesn't grab headlines. It won't spark controversy. In fact, when self-control is functioning properly, it helps people avoid scandal and embarrassment. It's an invisible virtue, operating behind the scenes to sustain a healthy, holy life.

And that's why I was wrong to sell it short. Self-control is foundational. It leads to freedom and flourishing. Ultimately, it's what allows a person to live a life that blesses others and glorifies God.

I dedicated this book to my son. The reason is simple. When I think of the hopes and fears I have for his life, they all come back to self-control. I want him to grow in his walk with God. I want him to be respectful and kind. I want him to study hard in school. As he enters his teen years, I want him to avoid the entanglements of sexual sin and bad influences. I want him to overcome the inertia of laziness that besets many young men and work hard to establish a career. One day, I hope to see him become a faithful husband and devoted father. When he stumbles along the way (which he inevitably will), I want him to experience God's forgiveness and start afresh. It will all take self-control. It will mean sidestepping a thousand temptations and distractions to pursue God's purpose for his life. It will demand following hard after Jesus. It won't be easy. But that's my prayer for him.

It's my prayer for you too.

Information alone isn't enough to bring about change. But I pray you'll take what you've read here and put it into action. Place God at the center of your life. Flee temptation. If you can't flee it, stand and fight. Eliminate distractions. Set sanctified goals. Grow your willpower. Break bad habits and replace them with healthy ones. Wage holy war on your sin. And above all, stay connected to God. As you do, you will see the fierce fruit of self-control begin to flourish.

No, self-control isn't the sexiest topic, but it's vital. Cultivating it will not only improve your own life. It will bless the lives of everyone you know and love. So endeavor to live a life marked by self-control. Your future self will thank you. And others will too.

Acknowledgments

Writing a book is rarely a solitary undertaking. Most authors need a lot of help to cross the finish line, and I'm no exception. I want to thank the people who inspired me to keep plodding along.

My wife, Grace: You read each chapter, gave constructive criticism, and pulled me out of the pit of doubt and self-loathing more than once. This book would have been impossible without you. You're an angel with a terrible disguise.

My family: To my parents (Art and Margee), in-laws (Brian and Jane), and all my siblings, both by birth and marriage (David, Sonya, Darren and Tiffany, Dan and Christa, Jason and Faith, Nathanael and Kerri, Cory and Antoinette), you've all been incredibly supportive and many of you helped me pick the title and sort through cover options. Thank you.

My friends: Kyle Rohane, Brandon O'Brien, Paul Pastor, Dan Darling, Kevin Emmert, Duane Sherman, Amy Simpson, Kevin Miller, Skye Jethani, Jody Jasurda—you were all kind enough to discuss the ideas in this book with me and offer valuable input. Marshall Allen, friend and agent extraordinaire, thanks for the hours of dreaming and scheming about this project. It wouldn't have happened without you.

The experts: Thanks for sharing your research and insights with me. Brad Wright, Sarah Schnitker, and Bill Russell, you were especially helpful and patient. I hope I haven't oversimplified or misrepresented your research.

The Moody team: Randall Payleitner, thanks for catching the vision for this book and championing it. Connor Sterchi, this book is much better because of your thoughtful and thorough edit. Erik Peterson, thanks for a great cover. Jeremy Slager and Kathryn Eastham, thanks for spreading the word! To all my godly and brilliant colleagues at Moody Publishers, I'm honored to serve alongside you.

Jesus: For saving me, and for refusing to let me remain the same, thank you. I will be eternally grateful.

Notes

Introduction: A Foundation for the Soul

1. Eusebius, *Eusebius: The Church History*, trans. Paul L. Maier (Grand Rapids: Kregel Academic, 2007), 65.
2. *The Library of Original Sources*, vol. 3, ed. Oliver J. Thatcher (Milwaukee: University Research Extension Co., 1907), 365.
3. Eusebius, *Eusebius: The History of the Church*, trans. G. A. Williamson (New York: Penguin Classics, 1965), 52.
4. John Rickaby, "Cardinal Virtues," *Catholic Encyclopedia* (2003 Online Edition).
5. @ThriveCenter. "Self control is an instrumental virtue. It facilitates the acquisition/development of other virtues: joy, gratitude, generosity," May 25, 2017, https://twitter.com/ThriveCenter/status/867798157496733696.

Chapter 1: Why Self-Control?

1. *The Anti-Pelagian Works of Saint Augustine*, vol. 1, trans. Peter Holmes, ed. Marcus Dods (Edinburgh: T&T Clark, 1989), 319.
2. Walter Mischel, *The Marshmallow Test: Why Self-Control Is the Engine of Success* (New York: Back Bay Books, 2015), 4–5.
3. Augustine, *The Confessions: With an Introduction and Contemporary Criticism*, trans. Maria Boulding, ed. David Vincent Meconi (San Francisco: Ignatius Press, 2012), 213.
4. Owen Strachan, October 30, 2017, https://www.facebook.com/ostrachan.
5. Annie Dillard, *The Writing Life* (New York: Harper Perennial, 2013), 32.
6. Justin Taylor, "The Incredible Testimony as a Former Gymnast Confronts Her Sexual Abuser in Court," The Gospel Coalition, January, 24, 2018, https://www.thegospelcoalition.org/blogs/justin-taylor/incredible-testimony-former-gymnast-confronts-sexual-abuser-court/.
7. Ibid.
8. HELPS Word-studies, https://biblehub.com/greek/1466.htm.
9. Kenneth Wuest, *Word Studies From the Greek New Testament*, vol. 2 (Grand Rapids: Eerdmans, 1980), 46.
10. Kelly McGonigal, *The Willpower Instinct: How Self-Control Works, Why It Matters, and What You Can Do to Get More of It* (New York: Avery, 2012), 9.

Chapter 2: Sorry, Self-Control Isn't About You

1. Clayton M. Christensen, "How Will You Measure Your Life?," *Harvard Business Review*, July/August 2010, https://hbr.org/2010/07/how-will-you-measure-your-life.
2. Ibid.
3. Ibid.
4. Augustine, *The Confessions: With an Introduction and Contemporary Criticism*, trans. Maria Boulding, ed. David Vincent Meconi (San Francisco: Ignatius Press, 2012), 213.
5. Tim Keller, *Making Sense of God: An Invitation to the Skeptical* (New York: Viking, 2016), 89.

6. Ibid., 90.
7. Augustine, *Confessions*, trans. Henry Chadwick (New York: Oxford University Press, 2008), 3.
8. Sir Alec Patterson, *Leadership Journal 1, no. 2*, http://www.preachingtoday.com/illustrations/1996/april/1399.html.
9. John Piper, "The Fierce Fruit of Self-Control," Desiring God, May 15, 2001, https://www.desiringgod.org/articles/the-fierce-fruit-of-self-control.
10. John Tierney, "For Good Self-Control, Try Getting Religious About It," *The New York Times*, December 29, 2008, https://www.nytimes.com/2008/12/30/science/30tier.html.
11. Michael E. McCullough, quoted in ibid.
12. Michael E. McCullough and Brian L. B. Willoughby, "Religion, Self-Regulation, and Self-Control: Associations, Explanations, and Implications," *Psychological Bulletin* 135, no. 1 (2009): 72.
13. Ibid., 78.
14. Francois Mauriac, *What I Believe* (London: Forgotten Books, 2018), as quoted by Philip Yancey in *The Jesus I Never Knew* (Grand Rapids: Zondervan, 1995), 118.
15. Ibid.
16. Thomas Chalmers, "The Expulsive Power of a New Affection" (sermon), date unknown, www.theologynetwork.org.

Chapter 3: Meeting the Enemies

1. Marguerite Shuster, *What We Have Become as Sinners* (Grand Rapids: Eerdmans, 2004), 164; quoted in Cindy Crosby, "An Unpopular Topic," *Christianity Today*, June 1, 2004, 64, https://www.christianitytoday.com/ct/2004/june/15.64.html.
2. "New Research Explores the Changing Face of Temptation," Barna Group, January 25, 2013, https://www.barna.com/research/new-research-explores-the-changing-shape-of-temptation/.
3. Ibid.
4. David Brooks, *The Road to Character* (New York: Random House, 2015), 11.
5. Ibid., 15.
6. Ibid., 11.
7. Ibid., 263.
8. Ibid., 263–64.
9. Ibid., 264.

Chapter 4: Hope for Growth

1. Kelly McGonigal, *The Willpower Instinct: How Self-Control Works, Why It Matters, and What You Can Do to Get More of It* (New York: Avery, 2012), 17.
2. Roy F. Baumeister et al., "Ego Depletion: Is the Active Self a Limited Resource?," *Journal of Personality and Social Psychology* 74, no. 5 (1998): 1254.
3. Ibid., 1252.
4. Roy F. Baumeister, quoted in John Tierney, "Why You Need to Sleep On It," *The 6th Floor* (blog), *New York Times*, August 17, 2011, https://6thfloor.blogs.nytimes.com/2011/08/17/why-you-need-to-sleep-on-it/?_r=0.
5. Bradley Wright and David Carreon, "The Science of Sinning Less: What New Research Reveals about Self-Control and Willpower," *Christianity Today*, April 21, 2017.

6. Colin Robertson, "The Hot-Cold Gap: How We Set Ourselves Up For Willpower Failure," Willpowered, October 20, 2014, http://www.willpowered.co/learn/the-hot-cold-empathy-gap.
7. Hal Ersner-Hershefield, G. Elliott Wimmer, and Brian Knutson, "Saving for the Future Self: Neural Measures of Future Self-Continuity Predict Temporal Discounting," *Social Cognitive and Affective Neuroscience* 4, no. 1 (March 2009): 85–92.
8. McGonigal, *The Willpower Instinct*, 172.
9. Min J. Kang and Colin F. Camerer, "FMRI Evidence of a Hot-Cold Empathy Gap in Hypothetical and Real Aversive Choices," *Frontiers in Neuroscience*, June 10, 2013.
10. Michelle McQauid, interview with Roy Baumeister, "Can You Have More Willpower? Interview with Roy Baumeister," *From Functioning to Flourishing* (blog), *Psychology Today*, June 29, 2017, https://www.psychologytoday.com/us/blog/functioning-flourishing/201706/can-you-have-more-willpower.
11. Wright and Carreon, "The Science of Sinning Less."
12. McGonigal, *The Willpower Instinct*, 24.
13. Charles Stone, "3 Morning Habits Guaranteed to Boost Brain Power," Biblical Leadership, July 21, 2017, https://www.biblicalleadership.com/blogs/3-morning-habits-guaranteed-to-boost-brain-power/.
14. Malte Friese and Michaela Wanke, "Personal Prayer Buffers Self-Control Depletion," *Journal of Experimental Social Psychology* 51 (March 2014): 56–59.
15. https://www.goodreads.com/quotes/35269-i-have-so-much-to-do-that-i-shall-spend.

Chapter 5: The Transforming Power of Habits

1. Charles Duhigg, "Q&A with Charles DuHigg on The Power of Habit," February 2012, charlesduhigg.com/wp-content/uploads/2012/02/QA.doc.
2. Charles Duhigg, *The Power of Habit: Why We Do What We Do in Life and Business* (New York: Random House, 2012), 186.
3. Ken Kurson, "Surrender to Tim Ferriss: The Dynamo Behind the '4-hour' Books Should Run Your Life (And Maybe Our City)," April 2, 2013, http://observer.com/2013/04/surrender-to-tim-ferriss-the-dynamo-behind-the-4-hour-books-should-run-your-life-and-maybe-our-city/.
4. John Ortberg, *Soul Keeping: Caring for the Most Important Part of You* (Grand Rapids: Zondervan, 2014), 150.
5. Arthur V. Peterson Jr., "Hutchinson Smoking Prevention Project: Long-Term Randomized Trial in School-Based Tobacco Use Prevention—Results on Smoking," *Journal of the National Cancer Institute* 92, no. 24 (December 20, 2000): 1979–91.
6. David Brooks, *The Social Animal: The Hidden Sources of Love, Character, and Achievement* (New York: Random House, 2012), 126.
7. James K. A. Smith, *You Are What You Love: The Spiritual Power of Habit* (Grand Rapids: Brazos Press, 2016), 3.
8. Ibid.
9. A. W. Tozer, *The Knowledge of the Holy* (New York: HarperCollins, 1978), 1.
10. Smith, *You Are What You Love*, 6.
11. Todd Hunter, *Our Favorite Sins: The Sins We Commit and How You Can Quit* (Nashville: Thomas Nelson, 2012), 59.
12. Smith, *You Are What You Love*, 6.
13. Jerry Jenkins, "Precious Memories: Billy Graham (1918–2018)," https://jerryjenkins.com/precious-memories-billy-graham-1918-2018/.

14. https://twitter.com/john_starke/status/860137979976851456.
15. Alain de Botton, "Atheism 2.0," TED, July, 2011, https://www.ted.com/talks/alain_de_botton_atheism_2_0#t-556017.
16. Justin Taylor, "You Are What You Love: A Conversation with James K. A. Smith," The Gospel Coalition, April 5, 2016, https://www.thegospelcoalition.org/blogs/justin-taylor/you-are-what-you-love-a-conversation-with-james-k-a-smith/.
17. Duhigg, The Power of Habit, 271.
18. C. S. Lewis, Mere Christianity (New York: HarperCollins, 1952), 132.
19. Quoted by Michael Card, Scribbling in the Sand: Christ and Creativity (Downers Grove, IL: IVP, 2004), 97.

Chapter 6: Training Your Elephant

1. Benjamin Franklin, The Autobiography of Benjamin Franklin, 38, http://www.ushistory.org/franklin/autobiography/.
2. Ibid.
3. Ibid., 40.
4. Ibid., 38.
5. Ibid., 39.
6. Ibid.
7. Ibid., 41.
8. Ibid.
9. Jared Sparks, The Works of Benjamin Franklin (New York: Wiley and Putnam, 1844), 597.
10. Hal E. Hershfield et al., "Increasing Saving Behavior Through Age-Progressed Renderings of the Future Self," Journal of Marketing Research 48 (November 2011), https://www.ncbi.nlm.nih.gov/pmc/articles/PMC3949005/.
11. Jonathan Haidt, The Happiness Hypothesis: Finding Modern Truth in Ancient Wisdom, (Basic Books, 2006).
12. Taken from "A Mini Guide to Forming Habits," The Mindful Company, March 10, 2017, https://www.mindful-company.com/blogs/notebook/a-mini-guide-to-forming-habits. Image used by permission.
13. Live Science Staff, "People-Pleasers Eat More at Parties," Live Science, February 1, 2012, https://www.livescience.com/18235-people-pleasers-overeating-social-situations.html.
14. Charles Duhigg, "How Companies Learn Your Secrets," The New York Times, February 16, 2012, https://www.nytimes.com/2012/02/19/magazine/shopping-habits.html.
15. Ibid.
16. Richard H. Thaler and Cass R. Sunstein, Nudge: Improving Decisions about Health, Wealth, and Happiness (New York: Penguin, 2009), 3.
17. Charles Duhigg, The Power of Habit: Why We Do What We Do in Life and Business (New York: Random House, 2012), 62.
18. Phillippa Lally, "How are habits formed: Modelling habit formation in the real world," European Journal of Social Psychology 40, no. 6 (October 2010): 998–1009.
19. John Ortberg, Soul Keeping: Caring for the Most Important Part of You (Grand Rapids: Zondervan, 2014), 151.
20. Duhigg, The Power of Habit, 101.
21. Steve Benna, "8 Keystone Habits That Can Transform Your Life," Business Insider, August 6, 2015, http://www.businessinsider.com/keystone-habits-that-transform-your-life-2015-8.

22. Jack Shitama, "How Keystone Habits Help Me Grow as a Spiritual Leader," *BeADisciple* (blog), June 28, 2017, http://www.beadisciple.com/blog/how-keystone-habits-help-me-grow-as-a-spiritual-leader/.
23. Greg L. Hawkins and Cally Parkinson, *Move: What 1,000 Churches Reveal about Spiritual Growth* (Grand Rapids: Zondervan, 2016), 19, 275.
24. Quoted in "Remembering John R.W. Stott on His Birthday—One of the Greatest Evangelicals of Our Time," Verticallivingministries.com, April 27, 2012, https://verticallivingministries.com/tag/john-piper-on-john-stott/.
25. Tyler VanderWeele, quoted in Alan Mozes, "Devout Women May Enjoy Better Health," HealthDay, May 16, 2016, https://consumer.healthday.com/public-health-information-30/religion-health-news-577/organized-religion-might-boost-women-s-survival-710987.html.
26. Tyler J. Vanderweele and John Siniff, "Religion May be a Miracle Drug," October 26, 2016, https://www.usatoday.com/story/opinion/2016/10/28/religion-church-attendance-mortality-column/92676964/.
27. T. M. Luhrmann, "The Benefits of Church," *The New York Times*, April 20, 2013, https://www.nytimes.com/2013/04/21/opinion/sunday/luhrmann-why-going-to-church-is-good-for-you.html.
28. Laura Sessions Stepp, "Religion Has Been Found to Be Beneficial for Teens," *The Washington Post*, April 17, 2004, https://products.kitsapsun.com/archive/2004/04-17/450987_religion_has_been_found_to_be_b.html.
29. David Mathis, "Your Single Most Important Habit," Desiring God, March 6, 2016, https://www.desiringgod.org/articles/your-single-most-important-habit.
30. Mike Cosper, "Faith Mapping: An Interview with Mike Cosper," interview by Jason Vernon, Tony Morgan Live, March 27, 2013, https://tonymorganlive.com/2013/03/27/faith-mapping/.
31. Karen Ehman, *Let. It. Go.: How to Stop Running the Show and Start Walking in Faith* (Grand Rapids: Zondervan, 2012), 165.
32. Darryl Dash, *How to Grow: Applying the Gospel to All of Your Life* (Chicago: Moody, 2018), 109.
33. Ibid., 110.

Chapter 7: Grace Means I Don't Need Self-Control

1. Andrew Naselli, *Let Go and Let God?: A Survey and Analysis of Keswick Theology* (Bellingham, WA: Lexham Press, 2017).
2. Billy Graham, 1957, New York Crusade, embedded video, Justin Taylor, "60 Years Ago: Billy Graham's Madison Square Garden Crusade—An Interview with Grant Wacker," The Gospel Coalition, May 15, 2017, https://www.thegospelcoalition.org/blogs/evangelical-history/billy-grahams-madison-square-garden-campaign-60-years-later/.
3. Kevin DeYoung, *The Hole in Our Holiness: Filling the Gap Between Gospel Passion and the Pursuit of Godliness* (Wheaton, IL: Crossway, 2012), 90.
4. Ibid., 28.
5. John Ortberg, *The Life You've Always Wanted: Spiritual Disciplines for Ordinary People* (Grand Rapids: Zondervan, 1997), 46.
6. Dallas Willard, "Live Life to the Full," *Christian Herald* (U.K.), April 14, 2001, http://www.dwillard.org/articles/individual/live-life-to-the-full.
7. Todd Hunter, *Our Favorite Sins: The Sins We Commit and How You Can Quit* (Nashville: Thomas Nelson, 2012), 5.
8. Willard, "Live Life to the Full."
9. Francesca Gino, "Is It the Right Time for a Fresh Start? Help is here for all

those faltering New Year's Resolutions," Scientific American, March 1, 2016, https://www.scientificamerican.com/article/is-it-the-right-time-for-a-fresh -start/.

10. Kelly McGonigal, quoted in an article by Paula Davis-Laack, "How The What-The-Hell Effect Impacts Your Willpower: Strategies to avoid giving up when you slip up," *Pressure Proof* (blog), *Psychology Today*, January 31, 2017, https://www.psychologytoday.com/blog/pressure-proof/201701/ how-the-what-the-hell-effect-impacts-your-willpower.

11. Richard Brodie, "Mary Ainsworth and Attachment Theory," https://www. scribd.com/document/195116666/Mary-Ainsworth-and-Attachment-Theory.

12. Diane Benoit, "Infant-parent attachment: Definition, types, antecedents, measurement and outcome," *Pediatrics & Child Health* 9, no. 8 (November 2014): 541–45.

13. Matt Bradshaw, Christopher G. Ellison, and Jack P. Marcum, "Attachment to God, Images of God, and Psychological Distress in a Nationwide Sample of Presbyterians," *The International Journal for the Psychology of Religion* 20, no. 2 (2010): 130–47.

14. Alyssa M. Strenger, "The Moderating Effects of Attachment to God on Disordered Eating Behaviors," *Dissertation Abstracts International*, 2015.

15. Chris Norton, "Leaders and Friends Remember John Stott," *Christianity Today*, July 29, 2011, https://www.christianitytoday.com/ct/2011/julyweb-only/johnstottroundup.html.

16. Ibid.

17. Everett Rosenfeld, "Fond Farewells: John Stott, Theologian, 90," *Time*, December 14, 2011, http://content.time.com/time/specials/packages/article /0,28804,2101745_2102136_2102268,00.html.

18. Tim Stafford, "John Stott Has Died," *Christianity Today*, July 27, 2011, http:// www.christianitytoday.com/ct/2011/julyweb-only/john-stott-obit.html.

19. Fred Smith, "David Brooks: A Holy Friend," October 2, 2014, https://the-gathering.com/david-brooks-holy-friend/.

20. Ibid.

21. Ibid.

22. John Stott, "A Vision for Holiness," Preaching Today, Tape No. 94, https:// www.preachingtoday.com/sermons/sermons/2005/august/094.html.

23. "John Stott's Last Words of Advice," PreachingToday.com, May 14, 2015, https://www.preachingtoday.com/illustrations/2015/may/5051115.html.

24. Sophie DeMuth, "Whole30 and the Counter-Cultural Nature of Self-Discipline," https://christandpopculture.com/whole30-and-the-counter -cultural-nature-of-self-discipline/.

25. Ibid.

26. Hunter, 213.

Chapter 8: Disciplined Living in an Age of Distraction

1. John Koblin, "How Much Do We Love TV? Let Us Count the Ways," *New York Times*, June 30, 2016, https://www.nytimes.com/2016/07/01/business/ media/nielsen-survey-media-viewing.html.

2. Jacqueline Howard, "Americans Devote More Than 10 Hours a Day to Screen Time, and Growing," CNN.com, July 29, 2016, http://www.cnn.com /2016/06/30/health/americans-screen-time-nielsen/index.html.

3. Jayson Maclean, "Households Now Use an Average of Seven Connected Devices Every Day: Report," August 25, 2016, https://www.cantechletter

.com/2016/08/households-now-use-average-seven-connected-devices-every-day-report/.

4. Alexander Roberts and James Donaldson, *The Apostolic Fathers with Justin Martyr and Irenaeus* (Grand Rapids: Eerdmans, 1988), chapter XIV.

5. https://twitter.com/ahc/status/880407602580123648.

6. Ali Drucker, "Here's Exactly How Many Hours of Porn People Watched in 2015," Maxim, January 6, 2016, https://www.maxim.com/maxim-man/how-much-porn-do-people-watch-2016-1.

7. Brandon D. Smith, "Farewell, Social Media," Patheos, July 1, 2017, http://www.patheos.com/blogs/brandondsmith/2017/07/farewell-social-media/.

8. Ibid.

9. Ibid.

10. @StephenFurtick, "One reason we struggle w/ insecurity: we're comparing our behind the scenes to everyone else's highlight reel," May 10, 2011, https://twitter.com/stevenfurtick/status/67981913746444288.

11. C. S. Lewis, *The Screwtape Letters* (London: Macmillan, 1962), ix.

12. Philip Yancey, "Reading Wars," PhilipYancey.com, July 20, 2017, https://philipyancey.com/reading-wars.

13. Ibid.

14. "E-mails 'hurt IQ more than pot,'" April 22, 2015, CNN.com, http://www.cnn.com/2005/WORLD/europe/04/22/text.iq/.

15. Mike Allen, "Sean Parker unloads on Facebook: 'God only knows what it's doing to our children's brains,'" Axios, November 9, 2017, https://www.axios.com/sean-parker-unloads-on-facebook-god-only-knows-what-its-doing-to-our-childrens-brains-1513306792-f855e7b4-4e99-4d60-8d51-2775559c2671.html.

16. James Olds, Peter Milner, "Positive reinforcement produced by electrical stimulation of septal area and other regions of rat brain," *Journal of Comparative and Physiological Psychology* 47, no. 6 (December 1954): 419–27.

17. Susie East, "Teens: This Is How Social Media Affects Your Brain," CNN.com, August 1, 2016, https://www.cnn.com/2016/07/12/health/social-media-brain/index.html.

18. Eric Andrew-Gee, "Your smartphone is making you stupid, antisocial and unhealthy: So why can't you put it down?," *The Globe and Mail*, January 6, 2018, updated April 10, 2018, https://www.theglobeandmail.com/technology/your-smartphone-is-making-you-stupid/article37511900/.

19. Kelly McGonigal, "The Science of Willpower: Kelly McGonigal at TEDxBayArea," TEDx Talks, YouTube, May 18, 2012, https://www.youtube.com/watch?v=W_fQvcBCNbA.

20. Kelly McGonigal, *The Willpower Instinct: How Self-Control Works, Why It Matters, and What You Can Do to Get More of It* (New York: Avery, 2012), 127.

21. Chamath Palihapitiya, quoted in Amy B. Wang, "Former Facebook VP Says Social Media Is Destroying Society with 'Dopamine-Driven Feedback Loops,'" *Washington Post*, December 12, 2017, https://www.washingtonpost.com/news/the-switch/wp/2017/12/12/former-facebook-vp-says-social-media-is-destroying-society-with-dopamine-driven-feedback-loops/?noredirect=on&utm_term=.dcfcad54a508.

22. Laura M. Holson, "Putting a Bolder Face on Google," *New York Times*, February 28, 2009, https://www.nytimes.com/2009/03/01/business/01marissa.html?mtrref=www.google.com&gwh=A9C1B34992829EE9D36225DBD3C310D0&gwt=pay.

23. Clifford Nass, "Does Multitasking Lead to a More Productive Brain?," interview by Ira Flatow, NPR, June 11, 2010, https://www.npr.org/2013/05/10/182861382/the-myth-of-multitasking.

24. Tony Reinke, *12 Ways Your Phone Is Changing You* (Wheaton, IL: Crossway, 2017), 85.

25. Ibid., 144.

26. C. J. Coffee, "Sermon: 1 Thessalonians 4:1-8 – Part 2 – Pornography," December 10, 2017, http://www.thewellchurch.com/sermons/1-thessalonians-41-8-part-2-pornography/.

27. Ibid.

28. Brett McCracken, designed by Jeremy Hamann, "The Wisdom Pyramid," August 13, 2017, https://www.brettmccracken.com/blog/2017/8/3/the-wisdom-pyramid. Used by permission of the author.

29. Betsy Mikel, "Former Google Designer Says 1 Simple Trick Can Curb Your Smartphone Addiction," *Inc.*, January 15, 2018, https://www.inc.com/betsy-mikel/former-google-designer-says-1-simple-trick-can-curb-your-smartphone-addiction.html.

30. A. J. Swoboda, *Subversive Sabbath: The Surprising Power of Rest in a Nonstop World* (Grand Rapids: Brazos Press, 2018), 100.

Chapter 9: Learning from Addicts

1. John, "I Am an Addict," *Time*, March 5, 2018. 21.

2. "Dope Sickness," Detox to Rehab, https://detoxtorehab.com/dope-sickness.

3. "Definition of Addiction," ASAM, August 15, 2011, https://asam.org/resources/definition-of-addiction.

4. David DiSalvo, *What Makes Your Brain Happy and Why You Should Do the Opposite* (Amherst, NY: Prometheus Books, 2011), 88.

5. Elizabeth Scalia, *Little Sins Mean a Lot: Kicking Our Bad Habits Before They Kick Us* (Huntington, IN: Our Sunday Visitor, 2016), 5.

6. Lauren Brande, edited by Dan Wagener, "About the Alcoholics Anonymous (AA) 12-Step Recovery Program," created on May 14, 2018, modified on August 23, 2018, Recovery.org, https://www.recovery.org/topics/alcoholics-anonymous-12-step/.

7. Bill Wilson, "Step One," https://www.aa.org/assets/en_US/en_step1.pdf.

8. Kelly McGonigal, *The Willpower Instinct: How Self-Control Works, Why It Matters, and What You Can Do to Get More of It* (New York: Avery, 2012), 191.

9. Marco Battaglini, Roland Benabou, Jean Tirole, "Self Control in Peer Groups," *Journal of Economic Theory*, April 6, 2005, https://www.princeton.edu/~rbenabou/papers/JET2005%20pdf.pdf.

10. "The Twelve Steps of Alcoholics Anonymous," Alcoholics Anonymous (Great Britain), https://www.alcoholics-anonymous.org.uk/about-aa/the-12-steps-of-aa.

11. Charles Duhigg, *The Power of Habit: Why We Do What We Do in Life and Business* (New York: Random House, 2012), 68.

12. Ibid., 70.

13. Ibid., 71.

14. Ibid., 84.

15. Quoted in *The Westminster Collection of Christian Quotations: Over 6000 Quotations Arranged by Theme,* Compiled by Martin H. Manser (Louisville, KY: Westminster John Knox Press, 2001), 284.